Practical Physics

Dr. Patil Shriram B.
M.Sc. D.H.E. Ph.D
Associate professor,
Department of Physics,
S.S.V.P.S.L.K.Dr.P.R.Ghogrey Science College,
Deopur, Dhule
Maharashtra (India)
2015

Published By:

Wordit Content Design & Editing Services Pvt Ltd.
Newbridge Business Centre, C38/39, Parinee Crescenzo Building,
G Block, Bandra Kurla Complex, Bandra East,
Mumbai 400 051, India
T: +91 8080226699

Copyright © 2017 **Dr. Patil Shriram B.**

All rights reserved. Any unauthorized reprint or use of this material is prohibited. No part of this book may be reproduced or transmitted in any form or by any means, electronic or mechanical, including photocopying, recording, or by any information storage and retrieval system without express written permission from the author/publisher.

Please do not participate in or encourage piracy of copyrighted materials in violation of the author's rights. Purchase only authorized editions.

Copyright © 2017 Dr. Patil Shriram B.

Internationally Published

ISBN: 978-93-83952-65-6

Preface

I am very happy to place this book 'Practical Physics' in the hands of under graduate students, especially the students from North Maharashtra University, Jalgaon (Maharashtra, India). It is well known to us study in physics remains incomplete without the practical knowledge. This book is intended for the assistance of students and teachers in Physical Laboratories, to write out the practical details of the different experiments. Many of the experiments, however, which have been selected for description, require only very simple apparatus.

The general aim of the book is to place before the students a description of a course of experiments which shall not only enable him to obtain a practical associate with methods of measurement, but also as far as possible illustrate the more important principles of the various subjects. We have found it necessary to exclaim a considerable amount of more theoretical information.

We have made no attempt to give number of experiments but try to explain a few, the most typical experiments in each subject. Authors aim is to enable the student to make use of his practical work to obtain a clear and more real approaching into the principles of the subjects.

In compiling a book which is mainly the result of Laboratory experience, the author is indebted to friends and colleagues even to an extent beyond their own knowledge. Authors would gladly acknowledge a large number of valuable hints and suggestions.

I am especially indebted to the kindness of our Principal Dr. D.A.Patil who has always afforded me facilities for my academic developments. I am grateful to Prof. M.A.More for his constant support and encouragement. The author is thankful to his wife Surekha, son Dr. Rohan and daughter Dr. Shweta for rendering their assistance in the compilation and editing of the book. I am thankful to M/s Wordit Content Design and Editing services private (P) Limited Publishers, Mumbai, for their untiring efforts in bringing out the book with excellent printing and nice get up within the shortest possible time period.

In spite of grate care, some misprints and omissions might have crept in. I will be grateful to readers who will point them out. Suggestions for the improvement of the book are most welcome.

Author

Serial number	Name of experiment	Page number
	General Physics	
1	Moment of Inertia of a disc by torsional pendulum	07
2	Flat Spiral Spring	13
3	Surface Tension by Jaeger's method	18
4	Young's Modulus "Y" by Bending	22
5	Young's modulus by Vibration of a Cantilever	27
6	Viscosity by Poiseuille's method	31
7	Thermal conductivity by Lee's method	36
8	Bottle as a resonator	42
9	Velocity of sound by kundt's tube	45
10	Kater's Pendulum	49
	Electricity	
11	Frequency of A.C Mains.	53
12	Verification of Kirchhoff's Laws	57
13	Maximum Power Transfer Theorem	61
14	Charging and discharging of a condenser	63
15	Study of Analog Multimeter.	66
16	Verification of Thevenin's theorem.	71
17	Verification of Norton's Theorem.	74

Instrumentation

18	Study of Electric Energy Meter.	76
19	Energy gap of semiconductor diode.	81
20	I-V Characteristics of Photo cell.	85
21	Lissajous figure using C.R.O.	88
22	Thermistor characteristics.	90
23	Planks constant by photo cell.	93
24	Comparison of luminous intensities	97
25	Use of C.R.O.	99
26	Platinum resistance thermometer.	105

Light

27	Refractive Index of Prism.	108
28	Beam divergence of the laser.	114
29	Wavelength of the LASER source.	117
30	Double refracting prism.	121
31	I-V Characteristics of Solar cell.	126
32	Resolving power of grating.	131
	Appendix	xx

1. Moment of Inertia of a disc by torsional pendulum

The torsional pendulum is an interesting example of simple harmonic motion. It is helpful in explaining the meaning of moment of inertia and moment of torsion and how they affect the period of vibration. The one end of suspension wire hangs from a rigid support with the help of a chuck nut and the other end is clamped to a solid metallic disc of appropriate dimensions, usually 10 cm in diameter and 1 cm in thickness with the help of a chuck nut. A heavy metal ring of the same metal and the same outside diameter as the disc is included. When ring is placed on the disc, the moment of inertia, and therefore the period of vibration of the system, is increased.

According to Newton's first law of motion everybody offers a resistance to any change in its state of rest or uniform motion, unless it is compelled by externally impressed force, to change that state. This property of the body is known as inertia and it depends upon the mass of the body.

We know that, the moment of inertia of a body about an axis is defined as the sum of the products of the mass and the square of the distance of the particles from the axis of rotation. A body capable of rotation about an axis opposes any change in its state of rest or uniform angular rotation about that axis. The inertia in this case is known as rotational inertia or moment of inertia.

Consider a disc suspended from a rigid support, a fine metallic wire attached to its centre, as shown in figure. This arrangement is known as a torsional pendulum. The assumption is here that the torsion wire used is essentially an inextensible, but is free to twist about its axis. As the wire twists it rotates the disc in the horizontal plane. Let θ be the angle of rotation of the disc, and obviously when the disc is in rest position or when the wire is untwisted, then $\theta = 0$. Any twisting of the wire is inevitably associated with mechanical deformation. The wire resists such deformation by developing a restoring torque, τ which acts to restore the wire to its untwisted state. For relatively small angles of twist, magnitude of this torque is directly proportional to the angle of twist.

When a torsional pendulum is disturbed by applying the external force, from its equilibrium position i.e. when, $\theta = 0$, it executes torsional oscillations about this state at a fixed frequency, ω which depends only on the torque constant of the wire and the moment of inertia of the disk. Remember that the frequency is independent of the amplitude of the oscillation, assuming θ remains small enough. Torsional pendulums are often used for time-keeping purposes. For example the balance wheel in a mechanical wristwatch is a torsional pendulum in which the restoring torque is provided by a coiled spring. [1]

Aim: To determine the moment of inertia of a disc with the help of a ring.

Apparatus: A heavy disc suspended by a wire, a ring, stop watch, vernier calipers, telescope etc.

Figure:

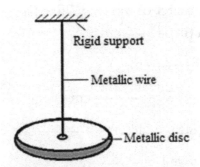

Figure: Experimental setup of Torsional pendulum

Formula: M.I of the disc I_0 is,

$$I_0 = I_1 \times \frac{T_0^2}{T_1^2 - T_0^2} \text{ gm.cm}^2$$

Where I_1 = Moment of inertia of the ring
= $M(R^2+r^2)/2$ gm.cm^2

T_0 = periodic time of the disc only.

T_1 = periodic time of the disc with ring.

Observations:

1. Least count of vernier caliper = 0.01cm.

2. Mass of the ring M = ------------ gm.

3. Internal diameter of the ring 2r = (i) -------- cm
   (ii) ------ cm (iii) --------- cm

   Mean 2r = --------- cm

   Hence radius "r" = ----------- cm

4. External diameter of the ring, 2R = (i)-------- cm
   (ii)------- cm (iii)--------- cm

   Mean 2R = --------- cm

   Hence radius "R" = --------- cm

Least count of stop watch = ------------- sec

Length of the wire L = ---------- cm

Observation table:

Obs. No.	System	Time for 10 Oscillations (t Sec)			Mean	Periodic time (Sec)
		1	2	3		
1	Disc					
2	Disc + ring					

Calculations:

Calculate the moment of inertia of the ring I_1, about an axis passing through its center and perpendicular to its plane using the formula given above. Then calculate I_0.

Procedure:

1. Find the least count of vernier calipers. Measure the internal and external diameters of the given ring. Hence calculate "r" and "R".

2. The radius of the suspension wire is measured using a screw gauge.

3. Suspend the disc and ring from the wire as shown in figure.

4. The length of the suspension wire is adjusted to suitable values like 0.3m, 0.4m, 0.5m ...0.9m, 1m etc.

5. Attach a paper pin (pointer) by means of wax to the rim of the disc.

6. Set the disc into torsion oscillations of small amplitude. Record the time for 10 oscillations. Take two more readings. Find mean t. hence determine periodic time I_0.

7. Place the ring coaxially on the disc and repeat the procedure as above. Determine the periodic time T_1.

8. Calculate I_1, the M.I. of the ring about the axis of rotation.

9. Using the formula calculate the M.I. of the disc.

Results: The moment of inertia of the given disc about a vertical axis passing through its center of gravity = -------- ------ $gm.cm^2$

Viva-voce:

1. What is torsional pendulum?
2. Define moment of inertia of the body? On what factors does it depend?
3. What is the physical significance of moment of inertia?
4. What is the effect of the length of the wire on the periodic time?

2. Flat Spiral Spring

We all very well familiar with the Hooks law. The spring is a system which satisfied the Hooke's law. In practice the reaction is proportional to the displacement. The spring is in core a long piece of wire wound as a helix of a certain diameter and a certain pitch. The spring when attached to a rigid support and loaded with appropriate weights on another end then lengthens on the side of the load. Ideally, if the load is much heavier than the spring then the elongation is uniform, it means that each turn lengthens by the same amount and the spring deforms as is shown in above figure. Since the spring is attached to the support, the upward reaction and the weight of the load form a couple and tender a torque which is clearly in the upward direction and proportional to the displacement. This happens for each coil and thus adds up, leading to the restoring torque. The restoring force is proportional to displacement, the difference between the lengths of the uninterrupted and the interrupted or disturbed spring. Since the upward reaction and the downward weight are tangential to the bulk of the wire, the material deforms in such a way that is regulate by the Stress-Strain relationship. This involves the modulus of rigidity of the wire which is usually characteristics of the structure of the material. [2]

Aim: To determine the modulus of rigidity (n) of the material of the wire of a flat spiral spring.

Apparatus: flat spiral spring, Micrometer screw gauge, Vernier calipers, stop watch, slotted weights with hanger etc.

Formula: Modulus of rigidity, η is given as,

$$\eta = \frac{16\pi^2 R^3 N}{r^4}\left[\frac{M+m/3}{T_1^2}\right]$$

Figure:

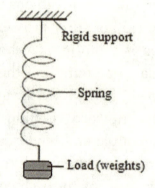

Figure : Experimental set-up to find modulus of rigidity

Observations:
- Least count of venire calipers = 0.01 cm.
- Outer Diameter of Spring 2R' =(i) -------- cm (ii) --------- cm (iii) -------- cm
- Mean 2R' = ------- cm
- Outer radius of spring (R') = 2R'/2 = --------- cm.
- Least count of micrometer screw = 0.001cm.

- Diameter of wire (2r) = (i) ---------- cm (ii) ---------- cm (iii) ---------- cm.
- Mean 2r = ----------- cm.
- Radius of wire (r) = 2r/2 = ------------ cm.
- Radius of spring measured to the center of the wire (R) = R' - r = -----cm.
- Total number of turns in the spring (N) =
- Mass of the spring (m) = 65 gm.
- Least count of stop watch = 1 sec.
- Length of the wire L = ---------------- cm.

Observation table:

Obs. No.	Mass attached M (gms).	M+ m/3 (gms)	Time for 10 oscillations (t sec)				Periodic time $T_1 = t/10$	$(T_1)^2$ Sec^2	$\dfrac{M+\frac{m}{3}}{T_1^2}$
			1	2	3	Mean			
1									
2									

Graph: plot the graph of $(T_1)^2$ against M.

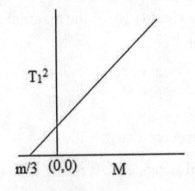

Procedure:

1. Count the number of turns of the flat spiral spring.

2. Measure the diameter of the wire of the spring using a micrometer screw gauge.

3. Measure the external diameter of the spring using a Venire calipers.

4. Clamp one end of the flat spiral spring to the rigid support of the stand and attach a slotted weight hanger to the lower end of the spring.

5. Attach a mass say 20 gm to the hanger. Apply a small force to the hanger in the downward direction so that there are vertical oscillations of small force to the hanger in the Measure the time for 10 oscillations. Take at least three readings.

6. Repeat the observations for different loads say 40gm, 60gm, 80gm……………..

7. Calculate periodic times for each load.

Results:

The modulus of rigidity (η) of the material of the wire of a flat spiral spring

η = -------------------- dyne/cm^2

Viva-voce:

1. Define the term elasticity.

2. Define modulus rigidity.

3. State the relation between Y, k and n.

4. What do you meant by periodic time?

5. In the present experiment if the diameter of the wire of the spring is reduced to half, what will be the effect on the modulus of rigidity?

3. Surface Tension by Jaeger's method

Surface tension is a phenomenon of the force of cohesion between molecules of a liquid. According to this characteristic of a molecular attraction, the free surface of a liquid acts as a thin membrane stretched over it. This membrane is under tension and trying to contract. Surface tension of liquid is defined as the "force per unit length acting on either side of a line drawn on the liquid surface in equilibrium, the direction of the force being tangential to the surface and perpendicular to the line".

There are many application of surface tension. Capillary rise is an outcome of surface tension. The blotting paper works on the capillary action. When water is used to wash the clothes and utensils, the detergent is adding in to the water to reduce the surface tension of water. [3]

Aim: To determine Surface Tension by Jaeger's method.

Apparatus: Jaeger's apparatus, capillary tube, glass beaker, adjustable stand, thermometer, Plastic scale, Travelling Microscope etc.

Figure:

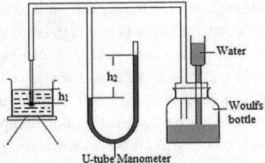

Figure: Experimental setup of Jaegers method

Formula:

$$\text{Surface Tension, } T = \frac{rg(h_1\sigma - h_2\rho)}{2} \text{ dynes/cm}$$

Observations:

1. Density of experimental liquid (water)
   $[\rho] = $ gm/cm^3.

2. Density of liquid (water) in the Manometer
   $[\sigma] = $ gm/cm^3

3. Diameter of the orifice of capillary tube
   $[d] = $ cm. Radius $[r] = $ cm

4. Temperature of experimental liquid = °C

Observation table:

Obs No.	Depth of orifice inside the liquid (h_2 cm)	Manometer reading Upper level A cm	Manometer reading Lower level B cm	h_1 = A−B cm	Mean h_1 cm
1	a = 2 cm				
2	b = 4 cm				

Practical Physics for undergraduates

Water is allowed to drip slowly into the large flask, so forcing bubbles of air out of the capillary tube which dips into a beaker of water. The lower end of the capillary tube is a depth h_1 below the water surface. It can be shown that the bubble will break free from the end of the tube when its radius is equal to the internal radius of the tube. Using a manometer the total pressure within the apparatus may be found; this is equal to the hydrostatic pressure ($h_1 \rho_1 g$) plus the excess pressure within the air bubble due to the surface tension of the water. The total pressure is given by the equation:

$h_2 \rho_2 g = h_1 \rho_1 g + 2T/r$ where ρ_1 is the density of water, ρ_2 the density of the liquid in the manometer, r the radius of the capillary tube and h_2 the difference in levels within the manometer.

Procedure:

1. Find the diameter of the orifice of the capillary tube using traveling microscope.

2. Arrange the apparatus as shown in figure. Clamp the capillary tube in a vertical position such that it will dip to the experimental liquid (water) kept in the beaker.

3. Adjust the resting stand of the beaker such that the depth of orifice in the water is h = say a cm. from the water level.

4. Open the stopcock of the dropping funnel slowly so that water falls slowly into the bottle and forces equal volume of air in to the tube ABCD. Adjust the flow of

water into the bottle so that an air bubble is formed at orifice in the water.

5. The pressure indicated by the manometer rises and become maximum when the bubble has a radius equal to the radius if the orifice.

6. Note down the readings of manometer levels before the bubble breaks.

7. Repeat the procedure for different values of h.

8. Note the temperature of the water in the beaker.

9. Calculate the surface tension using the given formula.

Results: The surface tension of water at-------- ⁰C is,
T = ------------dyne/cm

Viva-voce:

1. What are cohesive and adhesive forces? What do meant by surface tension?

2. What are the factors that affect the surface tension?

3. How does surface tension vary with temperature?

4. What is the difference in air bubble in liquid and a soap bubble?

5. In this experiment can we use mercury in the manometer?

4. Young's Modulus "Y" by Bending

When an external deforming force acts on a body, there may be change in the length, volume or shape of the body. As soon as the applied force remove, the body regains its original state more, less or completely. This property of a material of a body to regain its original state when the deforming forces are removed is called as elasticity.

The restoring force per unit area developed in the body is called Stress. Stress = F/a.

The ratio of change in dimensions to original dimensions is called as strain.

The Young's modulus is defined as the ratio of longitudinal stress to longitudinal strain within elastic limit. [4]

$$Y = \frac{Stress}{Strain} = \frac{F/a}{l/L} = \frac{FL}{al}$$

Aim: To determine the Young's modulus Y of a given material.

Apparatus: A uniform rectangular bar of the material (meter scale), two knife edges fixed on the rigid support, Hanger hook with pointer, slotted weights, traveling microscope, vernier calipers, micrometer screw gauge etc.

Figure:

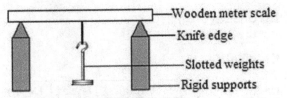

Figure: Experimental arrangement to find Y by bending

Formula:

$$Y = \frac{Mgl^3}{4bd^3e} = \frac{gL^3}{4bd^3}\left[\frac{M}{e'}\right] \text{ dynes/cm}^2$$

$$Y = \frac{gL^3}{4bd^3} \times \text{Slope dynes/cm}^2$$

Where, M – the mass attached,

e – depression for each mass.

e' – depression for constant mass say 150 gm.

Observations:

Length of the bar between the knife edges L = --------- cm

Least count of vernier calipers = 0.01cm.

Least count of micrometer screw = 0.001cm

Breadth of the Bar "b" = (i) ---------- cm (ii) ---------- cm
(iii) ---------- cm

Mean b = -------------- cm.

Depth of the Bar "d" = (i) ------------- cm (ii) ----------- cm
(iii) ---------- cm

Mean d = -------------- cm

Least count of Traveling Microscope = ------------ cm.

Observation Table:

Obs No.	Mass attached	Microscope reading			Depression for each mass (e)	Depression for (150gm) constant mass (e')	Mean e'
		loading	unloading	Mean			
1	0						
2	50						
3	100						

Procedure:

1. Find the least counts of vernier calipers and micrometer screw gauge. Measure the breadth and depth of the bar accurately at the different places of the bar.

2. Find the center of gravity of the given bar and put a marking line at this position. From this line of C.G. mark points of either side at equal distance (say 10cm) and draw sharp lines at these points.

3. Place the bar horizontally on the two knife-edges as shown in figure, such that it rests on the two marked lines. Suspend the hanger with pointer from the C.G. position.

4. Focus the microscope on the pointer so that its tip just touches the horizontal cross wire. Note this reading of microscope against zero mass attached.

5. Slowly insert 50 gm weight in the hanger. Adjust the micrometer screw on the top of the microscope so that it again touches the horizontal cross wire. Note this reading of the microscope.

6. Gradually increase the load in the steps of 50 and repeat the same procedure, note the microscope reading.

7. Now decrease the load in the steps of 50 gm and note down the unloading reading of microscope, starting from 250 gm to 0.

Graph: Plot the graph of depression for each mass (e) against mass attached (M).

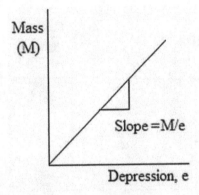

Results: Young's modulus of the given material (wood)

1. By observations, Y= ---------------------- dyne/cm^2

2. By graph, Y= ---------------------- dyne/cm^2

Viva-voce:

1. What is modulus of elasticity? Which is more elastic; rubber or steel?

2. How many modulus of elasticity do you know? State.

3. What is Young's modulus?

4. What do you meant by the term elastic limits?

5. What is depression?

6. What would be the change in Y if the breadth of the given bar is made double?

5. Young's modulus by Vibration of a Cantilever

A beam is defined as a structure of uniform cross section, whose length is large in comparison to its breadth and thickness. A cantilever is a uniform thin beam fixed in horizontal position at one end and loaded at the other end.

In this experiment we try to measure the Elasticity modulus of scales made of different materials with the cantilever beam arrangement. If we consider the beam in the position given in the figure below,

In this, by varying the mass suspended 'm' and get the Elasticity modulus of various materials. One can also vary the length of beam and get the behavior. [5]

Aim: To determine Young's modulus of a material of the beam by vibration method.

Apparatus: Wooden beam, Rigid clamps, slotted weights, stopwatch, Vernier calipers, Micrometer screw gage, etc.

Figure:

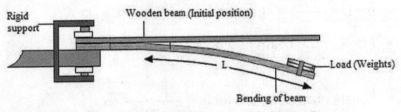

Figure: Experimental arrangement to find Youngs modulus by Bending

Formula:

$$Y = \frac{16\pi^2}{bd^3} \frac{l^3[M+\frac{33}{140}M_1]}{T^2} \text{ dynes/cm}^2$$

Observations:

- Least count of vernier calipers = 0.01 cm.

- Breadth (b) of the beam = (i) ---------- cm (ii) ----------- cm (iii) ----------- cm

- Mean b = -------------- cm

- Least count of micrometer screw =

- Thickness of the beam (d) =(i) -----------cm (ii) -------------cm (iii)----------cm

- Mean d = ----------- cm

- Length of the whole beam (L) = 100cm

- Length of the beam from the edge of the clamp to the free end (l) = 90 cm.

- Mass of the whole beam (m) = -------------- gm.

- Mass per unit length of the whole beam, m/L = ----------- gm/cm

- Mass of the beam of length 90 cm = M_1 = (m/L) l = ------------ gm.

- Least count of stop watch = ------------ sec.

Observation Table:

Obs No.	Mass attached	$M+\frac{33}{140}M_1$	Time for 50 vibrations	Periodic time (T) Sec	T^2	$\frac{1^3}{T^2}$	$\frac{1^3}{T^2}\left[M+\frac{33}{140}M_1\right]$

Procedure:

1. Measure the breadth and thickness of the given wooden bar using vernier calipers and the micrometer screw respectively.

2. Clamp the given wooden beam such that from the edge of the clamp to its free length, the length will be 90 cm.

3. Place 20 gm mass on the holder fixed at the free end of the beam.

4. Allow the beam to vibrate vertically with small amplitudes.

5. Measure the time required for 25 vibrations.

6. Increase the mass in the steps of 40, 60, 80, and 100. Repeat the above procedure.

7. Tabulate the observations and other factors in the observation table.

Calculations:

Results:

The Young's modulus of a material of the beam (wood) by vibration method is found to be Y = -------------- dyne/cm²

Viva-voce:

1. Define Cantilever.

2. If the dimensions of the given wood beam are doubled, the value of Y will be doubled/remain unchanged? Why?

3. What do you meant by restoring force?

4. What is the use of study of cantilevers?

6. Poiseuille's method

Viscosity is the property showed by fluids only. The flow of a liquid through a capillary tube is governed by the well known Poiseuilles equation,

$$V = \frac{\pi a^4 p}{8\eta L}$$

Where, 'V' is the volume of the liquid flowing per second, 'a' is the radius of the capillary and 'L' be the length of the capillary, 'P' is the pressure difference between the ends of the capillary tube and 'N' is the coefficient of the viscosity of the liquid. This equation is valid, when following two conditions are satisfied.

1. The flow should be streamline.

2. The flow should be such that the kinetic energy obtained by the liquid should be negligibly small.

Note that this formula reflects the physical equilibrium situation of a force on the fluid due to a pressure difference 'p' being balanced by a viscous force (i.e., one due to a frictional effect), with no other forces acting.

The flow of water, 'Q', is to be measured at different values of 'p' and for different capillary tubes. The pressure 'p' depends on the head of water, i.e., the height of the water in the reservoir above the level of the tube. The length of the tube can be readily found. The radius is more difficult to find. The viscosity of water changes rapidly with temperature. [6]

Aim: To determine the coefficient of viscosity of a given liquid flowing through the capillary tube.

Apparatus: Constant head apparatus with manometer, capillary tube, beaker, stop watch, measuring cylinder, meter scale, experimental liquid, etc.

Figure:

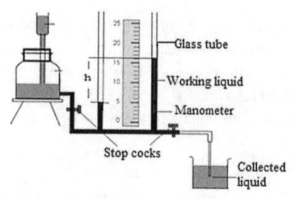

Figure: Experimental arrangement of Poiseuilles method

Observations:
- Radius of capillary tube, a = ----------- cm. Length of capillary tube, L = ----------- cm.
- Density of the experimental liquid (Water) i.e. ρ = 1gm/c.c.
- Room temperature = ⁰C.

Observations Table:

Obs No.	Manometer reading	$h = h_1 \sim h_2$	liquid collected in 2 min (M)	flow Rate of liquid $V = \dfrac{M}{60 \times 2}$	$\dfrac{h}{V}$	$\dfrac{h}{V}$ mean

Formula:

$$\eta = \frac{\pi a^4 \rho g}{8L} \times \left[\frac{h}{V}\right]_{mean} \quad \text{Poise} \qquad \eta = \frac{\pi a^4 \rho g}{8L} \times \text{Slope} \quad \text{Poise}$$

Graph:

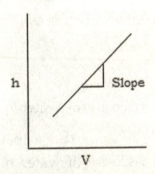

Procedure:

1. Arrange the apparatus as shown in figure. The experimental liquid is filled in the bottle of constant head apparatus.

2. Measure the length of capillary tube L.

3. Observe that the manometer liquid levels are equal. Adjust the stop cocks such that the manometer levels

shows some height difference say 1cm (i.e. $h_1 \sim h_2 = h$ = 1cm) and the water flows from the outlet is very slow. Note these readings of h_1 and h_2.

4. Collect the water in the beaker from the outlet, for the desired time say for 2 minutes.

5. Measure the volume M of collected water using measuring cylinder.

6. Repeat the above procedure for different height differences say h = 2, 3, etc.

7. Note the room temperature.

8. Formulate the complete observation table.

9. Calculate the coefficient of viscosity of water using the formula.

Results:

The coefficient of viscosity of water η = --------poise, at ------°C, by calculations,

The coefficient of viscosity of water η = --------poise, at --------- °C, by graph.

Viva-voce:

1. What do you mean by viscosity?

2. Define coefficient of viscosity of a liquid. State its units and dimensions.

3. State different types of flows.

4. Define streamline and turbulent flow?

5. Why the capillary tube of small bore is used?
6. Define poise.
7. What is the effect of temperature on viscosity?

7. Lee's method

Heat is a one form of energy; it is transferred by three different methods from one point to other that are conduction, convection and radiation. Thermal conductivity is the quantity of heat transmitted through a unit thickness in direction normal to a surface of unit area, due to a unit temperature gradient under steady state conditions. This inherent property is independent of the size, shape or orientation of the object of the material.

When heat is supplied to the metallic disc as per the arrangement shown in figure and achieved a steady state is condition, let θ_1 and θ_2 be the temperatures of metallic disc and wood disc. Therefore, the temperature difference between the two ends of bad conductor is taken as $(\theta_1-\theta_2)$. Therefore, the rate of heat conducted through the bad conductor (wood) is,

$$Q_1 = \frac{KA(\theta_1-\theta_2)}{d} \quad \text{————(A)}$$

Here 'd' is the thickness of the bad conductor and 'A' is the area of cross section of the disc. The rate of heat lost by the wooden disc to surrounding under steady state condition is,

$$Q_1 = ms\left(\frac{d\theta}{dt}\right)_{\theta_2} \quad \text{————(B)}$$

Where m be the mass of the wooden disc, C is the heat capacity of steel disc and dθ/dt is its rate of cooling at T_2. Taking into account equation A and B, we can write,

$$K = \frac{msd\left(\frac{d\theta}{dt}\right)_{\theta_2}}{A(\theta_1 - \theta_2)} \quad \text{---(C)}$$

By measuring, (dθ/dt) at θ_2 and obtaining the value $(\theta_1-\theta_2)$, the thermal conductivity of the wooden disc K can be determined. [7]

Aim: To determine the Thermal Conductivity of a bad conductor (say wood) by Lee's method

Apparatus: Lee's disc apparatus, two thermometers, Circular disc of bad conductor, Screw gauge, vernier calipers, stop watch, steam chamber etc. π

Figure:

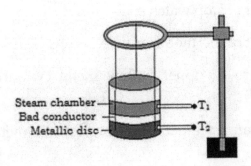

Formula:

$$\frac{msd\left(\frac{d\theta}{dt}\right)_{\theta_2}}{A(\theta_1-\theta_2)} \quad \text{i.e. } K = \frac{msd\left(\frac{d\theta}{dt}\right)_{\theta_2}}{\pi r^2(\theta_1-\theta_2)}$$

Observations:

Least count of venire caliper = 0.01 cm.

Diameter of bad conductor disc D = (i) -------- cm (ii) ----------cm (iii) --------- cm

Mean D = ----------- cm. Radius of bad conductor disc, r = ------------ cm.

Least count of micrometer screw = 0.001cm.

Thickness of bad conductor disc d = (i) ---------cm (ii) ---------cm (iii) --------cm

Mean d = ------------ cm.

Mass of the lower metallic disc m = ---------------- gm.

Specific heat of the metal of the metallic disc, S = ----------- cal/gm °C.

Least count of stop watch = ---------sec.

Least count of thermometer = ---------- °C.

Temperature of upper hollow metal cylindrical vessel θ_1 = °C.

Steady state temperature of lower metallic disc θ_2 = °C.

Observation Table: For cooling curve

Obs No.	Time in seconds	Temperature of metallic disc

Procedure:

1. Fill the steam chamber with water to nearly half and heat it to produce steam.

2. In the mean time, take weight of metallic disc by a weighing balance. Note its specific heat from a constant table. Measure the diameter of the specimen by a vernier caliper. Calculate the surface area, $A = \pi r^2$

3. Measure the thickness of the specimen by screw gauge. Take at least 5 observations at different places/spots and take the mean value of those readings.

4. Arrange the specimen, steam chamber etc. in position and suspend it from the clamp stand. Insert the thermometers.

5. As steam is ready, connect the boiler outlet with inlet of the steam chamber by a rubber tube.

6. Thermometers will show a rise in temperatures, observe the steady temperatures T_1 and T_2.

7. Wait for some time (10 minutes) and note the steady temperature and stop the steam flow.

8. Remove the boiler (stop the heat supply) and the specimen. Metallic disc is still suspended. Now the steam chamber and metallic disc are in direct contact with each other so that by the natural law of heat, both metallic disc and steam chamber will be in thermal equilibrium.

9. Remove the steam chamber and wait for 2 - 3 minutes so that heat is uniformly distributed over the metallic disc.

10. Now start to record the temperature at 1 minute intervals. Continue till the temperature falls by 30°C from the steady state temperature.

11. Plot the graph of temperature against the time and find dθ/dt at steady state temperature.

12. Find the thermal conductivity of the specimen using the given formula.

Graph: plot the graph of cooling curve. Find the slope dθ/dt at the steady state temperature θ_2.

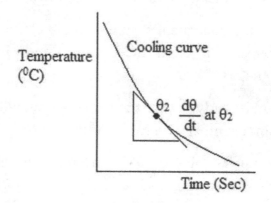

Results:

Thermal conductivity of the given bad conductor (wood) is,

K = --------------------cal/sec.cm². unit temperature gradient.

Viva-voce:

1. Which are the processes of heat transfer?

2. Define coefficient of thermal conductivity?

3. What is temperature gradient?

4. What do you meant by steady state?

5. Why it is necessary to obtain the steady state before taking the observations?

6. Can this method be used to good conductors? Why?

7. In the present experiment if the thickness of the bad conductor is reduced to half, what will be the effect on the thermal conductivity?

8. Bottle as a resonator

When air is blown across the opening of an object with a spherical cavity and a sloping neck, as shown in above figure, known as Helmholtz resonator and the resonance is known as Helmholtz resonance. Helmholtz resonance is given by the equation,

$$F = \frac{C}{2\Pi} \sqrt{[\frac{A}{VL}]}$$

Where, 'C' is the velocity of sound wave in the medium, 'L' is the length of the neck, 'a' is the area of cross section of the neck and 'V' is the volume of the air cavity. Helmholtz resonance is an oscillating wave system. Actually air is blown across the opening; the air in the neck flows inward and exerts a compression force inside the resonating bottle. Once compressed, air in the cavity then rebounds and flows out of the bottle, creating an environment inside the bottle with a pressure that is lower than that of the surroundings. Over compensation causes air to flow then flow back into the bottle creating an oscillating system. It is most commonly accepted that Helmholtz resonance is an accurate representation of all resonances in a cavity. [8]

Aim:
1. To verify the relation between the frequency and resonating volume of air using narrow necked resonator bottle.

2. To determine the unknown frequency of a turning fork as well as a neck constant.

Apparatus: A narrow necked resonator bottle, a set of turning fork, measuring cylinder, striking pad, beakers, water etc.

Observations:

Room temperature = --------°C.

Volume of the neck = ------ml.

Figure:

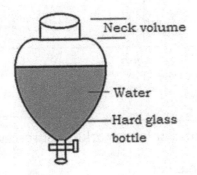

Observation Table:

Frequency of turning fork (Hz)(N)	Volume of the air column				N^2	$1/N^2$	N^2V
	V_1	V_2	V_3	Mean			

Formula:

$N^2(V+KV_0)$ = constant. Where, N –frequency of tuning fork, V- volume of resonating air

V_0 - the volume of neck, K= neck constant = neck correction factor.

Plot the graph of $1/N^2$ against Voltage V. From the graph, find out the value of unknown frequency, neck volume and 1/slope.

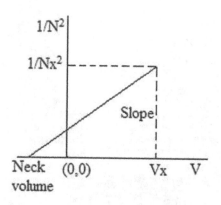

Viva-Voce:

1. What is the principle of working of resonator bottle?

2. What is resonance?

3. What do you mean by resonator?

4. Which types of waves produced in the air column of the resonating bottle?

5. In which form the wave's travels in air?

6. What is resonating length?

7. What is the function of water in the bottle?

8. What is velocity of sound in air?

9. Velocity of sound by kundts tube

In 1866, kundt showed that when standing waves were excited in a tube, dust particles in the tube will be arranged in periodic heap ups. Thus the nodes and antinodes can be detected by the characteristic canal vibration patterns of the dust or lycopodium powder as shown in the above figure. The wavelength can be obtained from distance between two successive nodes and antinodes (the distance between two successive nodes and antinodes in a standing wave is $\lambda/2$). Then the velocity of the sound can be calculated as $V = n\lambda$.

We know that, the sound waves in air are longitudinal waves and propagate in the form of compressions and rarefactions. These waves produce alternately the states of compression and rarefaction at a point in the medium. When two or more sound waves travel together, the superposition principle states that "the resultant wave at any point in the medium is the algebraic sum of the individual waves at that point".

As the result of interference between the longitudinal sound waves travelling in opposite directions in glass tube the standing waves can be set up. The phase relationship between the incident wave and the reflected from one end of the tube depends on whether that end of the tube is closed or open. If the tube is closed at one end, the closed end is a displacement node, because the wall at this end does not allow longitudinal motion of the air molecules. So that at the closed end the reflected wave will be out of phase by 'π' with the incident wave. As the pressure wave is π/2 out of phase with the displacement wave, the closed end will be pressure antinode. The open end of the air column is a displacement antinode and pressure node. The frequencies at which standing waves can be set up in an air column enclosed by a tube that is open at both at ends can be easily calculated. Because both ends are open, they should be pressure nodes and displacement antinodes. Therefore the length of the air column must be equal to an exact number of half wavelengths. [9, 10]

Aim: To calculate the velocity of sound in air by using Kundts tube.

Apparatus: Kundts tube, signal generator, horn unit, meter scale, fine saw dust or lycopdium powder.

Figure:

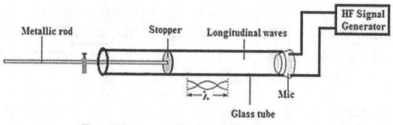

Figure: Experimental setup of Kundts tube

Formula:
Velocity of sound (V) = Frequency (n) X Wavelength (λ).

Frequency (Hz)	Distance between two successive nodes or Antinodes (λ/2) in cm.				λ (cm)	λ (m)	Velocity V= n λ
	I	II	III	Mean			
1000							
1500							

Procedure:

The apparatus consists of a transparent glass tube of length 70-80 cm. Distribute the cork dust uniformly over the entire length of the glass tube. Ensure that both the glass tube and cork dust must be dry. Connect the function generator, LF amplifier and the sound head. The sound head should be placed close to one of the glass tube.

Tune the frequency generator slowly. At a certain frequency, a standing wave will be present in the tube and can be visualized as periodic pileups of cork powder forms ripples or striations. This should not be confused with the nodes and antinodes. A sharp standing wave will be formed. At the antinodes point the air moves strongly and the powder particles are dispersed and can sediment only at node points. Measure the distance between two nodes or two antinodes, which will give half of the wavelength. Note down the frequency of the LF amplifier. Tune the frequency again so that a higher harmonic is obtained. Once the standing wave is observed, repeat the step 3. Care should be taken to distribute the cork dust uniformly over the entire length of tube after each measurement. Calculate the velocity of sound in air. Close one end of the tube and repeat the experiment.

Kundt's tube:
Viva-Voce:
1. Which elements are consists in the kundts tube experiment?
2. How waves are produced in the tube?
3. Which types of waves are produced in the kundts tube?
4. Is there any relation between the frequency and number of waves produced?
5. What is the principle of super position of waves?
6. What is the function of stopper?
7. What is the frequency of sound in the air?

10. Katers pendulum

The value of acceleration due to gravity i.e. 'g' can be determined Using a simple pendulum, by finding the period time 'T' and measuring the length of the pendulum i.e. 'L'. The value of periodic time 'T' can be finding with considerable precision by simply timing a large number of oscillations.

$$T = \sqrt{\frac{L}{g}} \quad \text{-----(1)}$$

The center of the mass is very hard to estimate where exactly it is. To overcome this difficulty one can turn a physical pendulum into a reversible (kater's) pendulum. Two knife-edge pivot points and two adjustable masses are positioned on the rod so that the period of oscillation is the same from either edge. The kater's pendulum used in the laboratory is diagramed above.

A physical pendulum is a rigid body oscillates in a vertical plane about any horizontal axis passing through the body. The resultant force acts through the center of mass. The time period of oscillation of the physical pendulum is related to the moment of inertia 'I' about the point of suspension.

$$T = 2\pi \sqrt{\frac{I}{mgl}} \quad \text{-----(2)}$$

Where m be the mass of the rigid body and l is the length between the point of suspension and the center of gravity.

Using the theorem of parallel axis, the moment of inertia 'I' can be expressed as,

$$I = MK^2 + Ml^2 \quad \text{------------} \quad (3)$$

Where k is the radius of gyration, therefore above equation takes the form,

$$T = 2\pi \sqrt{\frac{K^2+l^2}{mgl}} \quad \text{----------}(4)$$

The kater's pendulum has two pivot points on opposite sides of the centre of gravity from which the pendulum can be suspended. If 1_1 and 1_2 are the distance of the centre of gravity from pivot points 1 and 2 respectively. Following equation 4, the periodic time about 1 and 2 can be written as,

$$T_1 = 2\pi \sqrt{\frac{K^2+l_1^2}{mgl_1}} \quad \text{and} \quad T_2 = 2\pi \sqrt{\frac{K^2+l_2^2}{mgl_2}}$$

If the length l_1 and l_2 are so adjusted that, $t_1 = t_2 = t$, then one can write the above equation as,

$$T = 2\pi \sqrt{\frac{(l_1+l_2)r}{g}} \quad \text{Hence,} \quad g = 4\pi^2 \frac{(l_1+l_2)r}{T^2}$$

Then, $(l_1+ l_2)$ r is the equivalent length of the pendulum, which satisfies the condition of reversibility. [11]

Aim: To find the resonating length of Katers pendulum and the acceleration due to gravity.

Apparatus: Set up of Katers pendulum, Telescope, weights, meter scale, etc.

Observation table:

Obs No.	Length of simple pendulum L (cm)	Maximum amplitude A (cm)	Resonating length (cm)
1	60		
2	70		

Observation table for periodic time:

Obs no.	Time for 10 oscillation (t) sec	Periodic time T sec	Mean T
1			

Figure:

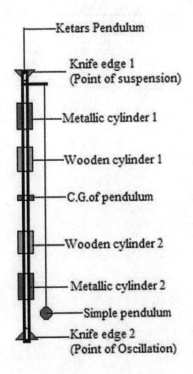

Formula:

$$g = 4\pi^2 \frac{L}{T^2}$$

Graph and result:

Graph of amplitude against length of pendulum gives resonating length of the pendulum.

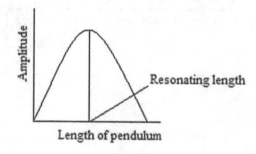

11. Frequency of A.C Mains

If a current carrying conductor is placed in a magnetic field perpendicular to the lines of force, a force begins to act on the conductor. The direction of the force is given by Fleming's left hand rule. If the current passing through the conductor is alternating, then the force reverses its direction in step with that of A.C. The conductor therefore experience a periodic force, which tends to set the conductor into vibrations. If the frequency of vibrations of the conductor equals the frequency of alternating current, resonance takes place and the conductor vibrates with maximum amplitude. When the amplitude of vibration is maximum the length of the vibrating wire is called as resonating length. This is the principle which is used to determine the frequency of A.C mains. [12]

Aim: To measure frequency A.C. mains using a sonometer and bar magnet

Apparatus: Sonometer with non-magnetic material wire, Bar Magnet pair, A.C. Voltage source, Slotted weights with hanger, meter scale

Practical Physics for undergraduates

Figure:

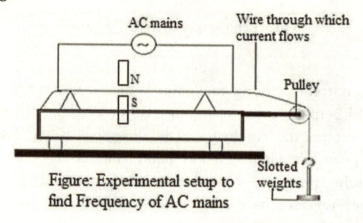

Figure: Experimental setup to find Frequency of AC mains

Formula:

$$\text{Frequency, } n = \frac{1}{\sqrt{\rho}} \times \frac{\sqrt{T}}{\lambda} \qquad \text{Frequency, } n = \frac{1}{\sqrt{\rho}} \times \text{Slope Hz}$$

Observations:

Mass per unit length i.e. Linear density of wire
$(\rho) = M/L = $ ------------ gm/cm

Least count of meter scale =   cm λ

Observation table:

Obs No.	Mass attached (m gm)	T = mg dynes	Resonating length (l cm) loading	Resonating length (l cm) Unloading	Mean (l cm)	$\lambda = 2l$	$\sqrt{T}$	$\sqrt{T}/\lambda$	Mean $\sqrt{T}/\lambda$

Graph:

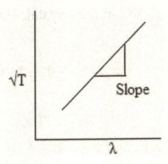

Procedure:

1. Go through the observations and fulfill them.

2. Set the apparatus as shown in figure. Stretch the wire with the minimum tension. Keep the two knife-edges C and D as far apart as possible.

3. Set two bar magnets on the two sides of the center of the wire with their opposite poles facing the wire as shown.

4. Connect the output of the A.C. source to the ends of the wire. Switch on the supply. The wire stats vibrating.

5. Move the knife edges C and D slowly towards each other so that the magnets always remain at the center of the wire.

6. Keep moving the knife-edges slowly till the wire vibrates with maximum amplitude.

7. Measure the distance between the two knife-edges.

8. Repeat the above procedure by increasing the tension in suitable steps.

Results:

1. The frequency of A.C. mains by calculations is
   (n) =   Hz

2. The frequency of A.C. mains by graph calculations is
   (n) =   Hz

Viva-voce:

1. What do you mean by the term A.C.?

2. What is meant by frequency of A.C.?

3. Why does the wire vibrate when the current is passing through it?

4. What is resonating length?

5. What is the effect of thickness (diameter) of wire on the results?

6. Does direct current also have any frequency?

7. In India what is the standard value of A.C. frequency?

Precautions:

1. There should be no twist in the sonometer wire.

2. Pulley should be frictionless.

3. Bar magnets should be placed in the middle of the wire.

4. Mass of the hanger should be included in tension T.

5. Alter the distance between the two bridges very slowly.

6. The diameter of the wire should be measured at various points.

12. Verification of Kirchhoff's Laws

Kirchhoff's Current Law: The algebraic sum of current or charge entering a junction is exactly equal to the charge leaving the junction, as it has no place to go except to leave. In short the algebraic sum of all the currents entering and leaving a junction must be equal to zero, i.e. Current (I) entering + Current (I) leaving = 0. This is also known as the the law of conservation of charge.

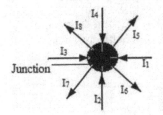

Current entering the junction $(I_1+I_2+I_3+I_4)$
= Current leaving the junction $(I_5+I_6+I_7+I_8)$
i.e. $I_1+I_2+I_3+I_4 +(-I_5-I_6-I_7-I_8) = 0$

Kirchhoff's Voltage Law: The law states that in any closed loop network, the total voltage around the loop is equal to the sum of all the voltage drops within the same loop which is also equal to zero. In other words the algebraic sum of all voltages within the loop must be equal to zero. This is also known as the law of conservation of Energy. [13]

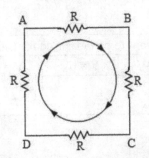

Around the loop, sum of all the voltsges is equal to zero
i.e. $V_{AB} + V_{BC} + V_{CD} + V_{DA} = 0$

Aim: To verify the Kirchhoff's Current & Voltage Laws.

Apparatus: Resistors, D.C. variable supply, D.C. Millimeter (0-50), D.C.

Circuit Diagram:

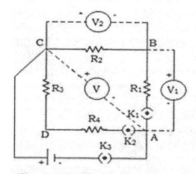 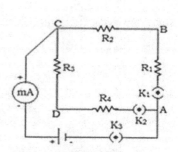

Figure (a) : Circuit diagram to verify Kirchoff's Voltage law

Figure (b): Circuit diagram to verify KIrchoff's current law

Observations:

Values of resistors by color code

R_1 = --------Ω R_2 = ---------- Ω

R_3 = --------Ω R_4 = ---------- Ω

Least count of voltmeter = ----- volts.

Least count of millimeter = ------mA.

Observation Table:
For Kirchhoff's Current Law:

Obs No.	Path	Current to be measured for (mA)		
		V = 4V	V = 6V	V = 8V
1	Branch ABC with K1 on	I_1 =	I_1 =	I_1 =

2	Branch ABC with K1 on	$I_2 =$	$I_2 =$	$I_2 =$
3	Path AC with K1 and K2 on	$I = I_1 + I_2 =$	$I = I_1 + I_2 =$	$I = I_1 + I_2 =$

Kirchhoff's Voltage Law:

Obs No.	Input voltage (volts)	Voltage measured across					
		A and B V_{AB}	B and C V_{BC}	A and C $V_{AC} = V_1 + V_2$	A and D V_{AD}	D and C V_{DC}	A and C $V_{AC} = V_3 + V_4$
1							
2							

Procedure:

For Kirchhoff's Current Law:

1. Connect the circuit as shown in circuit.

2. Adjust the power supply for any output voltage and then switch on the power supply.

3. Make the keys K_3 and K_1 on. Measure current I_1 that flows through the branch ABC.

4. Make the keys K_3 and K_2 on. Measure currant I_2 that flows through the branch ABC.

5. Make the keys K_3, K_1 and K_1 on. Measure current I that flows through the complete circuit ABCD. Verify $I = I_1 + I_2$.

6. Repeat the above procedure for 6V and 8V.

For Kirchhoff's Voltage Law:

1. Connect the circuit as shown in circuit 2. Do not connect the voltmeter.

2. Adjust the power supply for any output voltage and then switch on the power supply.

3. Make the keys K_3 and K_1 on. Measure the voltage V_{AB} between the point A and B, V_{BC} between the point B and C, V_{AC} between the point A and C. Verify $V_{AC} = V_{AB} + V_{BC}$.

4. Similarly make the keys K_3 and K_1 on. Measure the voltage V_{AD} between the point A and D, V_{DC} between the point D and C, V_{AC} between the point A and C. Verify $V_{AC} = V_{AD} + V_{DC}$.

5. Repeat the above procedure for 6V and 8V.

Results:

1. Kirchhoff's Current Law i.e. $I = I_1 + I_2$ is verified.

2. Kirchhoff's Current Law i.e. is verified.

Viva-voce:

1. State Kirchhoff's Laws

2. State Ohm's law

3. Can we apply Kirchhoff's laws for A.C. circuits? How?

4. What do you meant by the term 'Algebraic Sum'?

5. What are the conventions to connect ammeter and voltmeter in a circuit?

13. Maximum Power Transfer Theorem

Power delivered by the source of electro motive force i.e. EMF to the external resistance R_L is maximum when the external load, i.e. resistance 'R_L' is equal to the internal resistance 'R_i' of the source. This statement is known as maximum power transfer theorem.

Aim: To verify Maximum Power Transfer Theorem

Apparatus: Resistors, D.C. Power supply, Resistance box, multimeter, connecting wires.

Figure:

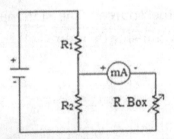

Figure: Circuit diagram for Maximum Power transfer theorem

Observation Table:

Obs No.	Load Resistance R_L Ohm	Current obtained		Power (Watt) $P = I^2 R_L$
		I (mA)	I (A)	

Procedure:

1. Connect the circuit as shown in the circuit diagram.

2. Switch on the power supply.

3. Take $R_L = 100\ \Omega$ resistance key from the resistance box. Note down the corresponding currents.

4. Repeat the procedure for different loads, i.e. $R_L = 200\Omega$, 300Ω, 400Ω, 500Ω, etc.

5. Calculate the power $I^2 R_L$ using the given formula.

6. Plot the graph power P against Load resistance R_L, note the load where power is maximum.

From the graph, note the external load resistance value for the maximum power. This value is equal to the internal resistance R_i of the source. This statement is known as maximum power transfer theorem. [14]

Graph:

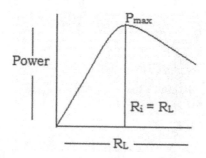

Results:

1. From the graph internal resistance (R_i) of the source =

2. As, $Ri = R_L$, maximum power transfer theorem is verified.

14. Charging and discharging of a condenser through resistor

A capacitor or condenser is a device consisting of two parallel plates separated by a dielectric material. It is used to store the charge, in electrostatic form. It is possible for dielectric materials such as air or paper to hold an electric charge because free electrons cannot flow through an insulator. However, the charge must be provided by some source. The capacitance of a condenser is measured in Farads.

There are two main effects observed with capacitors, charging and discharging. An applied voltage charges the condenser. The accumulation of charge results in building up of potential difference across the condenser plates and this is known as charging. The action of neutralization of charge by connecting a conducting path across the dielectric is known as discharging. In the discharging process the charge stored in condenser starts decaying. [15]

Aim: To determine the time constant of a RC circuit by charging & discharging of a condenser through resistance.

Apparatus: Electrolytic capacitor, resistor, D.C. power supply, Charging discharging key, D.C. micro ammeter (0–100A), stopwatch, connecting wires etc.

Circuit Diagram:

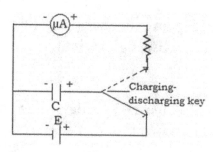

Formula: Time Constant (T) = 1.1RC

Where, R and C are values of resistor and capacitance used in the circuit.

Observations:

The value of resistor (R) = ---------- Ω.
The value of capacitor C = ------------ μF.

Observation Table:

Obs No.	Current through resistor (I μA)	Time of discharge of current (t Sec)			
		T_1	T_2	T_3	Mean T

Graph: Plot the graph of current (I) against (t) of discharging.

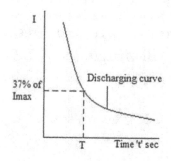

Procedure:

1. Connect the circuit as shown in the circuit diagram.
2. Check the polarities of capacitor, micro ammeter and battery.
3. Switch on the power supply.
4. Press the charging discharging key so that the capacitor gets charged to maximum value current.
5. Release the charging discharging key so that the micro ammeter would show maximum current I_{max}.
6. Repeat the above steps every time to measure the discharging key time to a particular decreasing value of current from I_{max}.

Results:

1. Theoretical value of RC time constant (-) is =   sec.
2. From the discharging curve, value of time constant (-) is   sec.

Viva-voce:

1. What is condenser?
2. State different types of condensers.
3. What is an electrolytic condenser?
4. What do you know by charging and discharging?
5. What is the unit of time constant? How?
6. Define the time constant of RC circuit.
7. Why the charging and discharging process is nonlinear?

15. Study of Analog Multimeter

Multimeters were invented in the early 1920s as radio receivers and other vacuum tube electronic devices became more common. The invention of the first multimeter is attributed to British Post Office engineer, Donald Macadie, who became dissatisfied with having to carry many separate instruments required for the maintenance of the telecommunications circuits. Macadie invented an instrument which could measure amperes, volts and ohms, so that the multifunctional meter was named as AVO meter (i.e. Ampere Volt and Ohm meter). The meter comprised a moving coil meter, voltage and precision resistors, and switches and sockets to select the range.

Multimeter is a very useful test instrument. By operating a multi-position switch on the meter they can be quickly and easily set to be a voltmeter, an ammeter or an ohmmeter. Thus multimeter is a device used for measurement of A.C., D.C. voltages, current and resistances.

Analog multimeter has pointer, which moves continuously along the scale, and the measurer reads the position of the indicator on the scale. In digital multimeter the measurement result is given in numerical form. An analog multimeter essentially consists of a sensitive moving coil galvanometer. It is provided with several scales on its dial, reading the current in amperes, potential difference in volts and resistance in ohms. [16]

Dr. Patil Shriram B.

Aim: To measure A.C and D.C. voltages, value of resistors, diode tests, continuity tests using an analog multimeter.

Apparatus: Analog millimeters, resistors, diode, A.C and D.C. variable voltages sources, A.C and D.C. voltmeters (0–25V), Electric Bulb etc.

Observation Tables:

1. D.C. Voltage Measurements:

Obs No.	Voltage measured by Voltmeter (V_v) Volts	Voltage measured by Multimeter (V_m) Volts	% Error

2. A.C. Voltage Measurements:

Obs No.	Voltage measured by Voltmeter (V_v) Volts	Voltage measured by Multimeter (V_m) Volts	% Error

3. Resistance Measurements:

Obs No.	Resistance measured by color code (R_c) Ohm	Resistance measured by Multimeter (R_M) Ohm	% Error

Procedure:

D.C. Voltage Measurements:

1. Set the position of the function switch on D.C. mode.

2. Insert the black test lead (Probe) in the common or (negative) socket and the red in the positive socket.

3. Set the range switch on 50V.

4. Switch on the D.C. Voltages carefully.

5. Connect the multimeter test leads to the output of the power supply. The polarities should be maintained properly.

6. Read the multimeter dial for D.C. Voltage carefully.

For the voltage below 10 volts the range switch should be set at 10V.

A.C. Voltage Measurements:

1. Set the position of the function switch on A.C. mode.

2. Insert the black test lead (Probe) in the common or (negative) socket and the red in the positive socket.

3. For A.C. voltage measurements the polarity is immaterial

4. Set the range switch on 50V.

5. Switch on the A.C. Voltages carefully.

6. Connect the multimeter test leads to the output of the power supply. The polarities should be maintained properly.

7. Read the multimeter dial for D.C. Voltage carefully.

For the voltage below 10 volts the range switch should be set at 10V.

Record all output voltages of the power supply by connecting a D.C. voltmeter of suitable range.

Resistance Measurements:
1. Find and record value of the resistance of the given resistors by colour code.

2. The resistance values of the same resistors are to be measured using multimeter as follows:

3. Set the position of the function switch on D.C. mode.

4. Connect the open metallic leads of the probes to each other. If the pointer of the multimeter does not stand at zero ohm position on the resistance scale, adjust the zero ohms switch till the pointer set at zero.

5. Adjust the position of the range switch. Connect the open leads of the probes to the ends of the resistors and note the reading of the pointer on the Ohms scale. Determine the resistance of the filament of the given bulb.

Testing of Diode:
1. Connect the forward bias circuit. Measure the forward resistance of the diode by connecting positive probe to the anode and negative of the probe to the cathode of the diode.

2. Connect the reverse bias circuit. Measure the reverse resistance of the diode by connecting positive probe to the cathode and negative of the probe to the anode of the diode.

Continuity Testing:
Connect the probe terminals at the appropriate positions in the circuit and note down the continuous and discontinuous points.

Results:
1. The working with multimeter is learned.
2. The A.C & D.C. voltages and resistance are measured using multimeter.
3. The diode testing & continuity testing is made using multimeter.

Viva-voce:
1. What is multimeter?
2. Give the ranges of the A.C voltage, D.C voltage and resistances.
3. Why it is necessary to make zero the zero of the resistance scale start from the extreme right hand side of the dial?
4. Why the adjustment of zero ohm is necessary before measuring a resistance value?
5. What is the difference between analog and digital multimeter.

16. Study of Thevenins theorem

Thevenin's Theorem: A two-terminal network can be replaced by a voltage source with the value equal the open circuit voltage across its terminals, in series with a resistor with the value equal to the equivalent resistance of the network.

Norton's Theorem: A two terminal network can be replaced by a current source with the value equal to the short circuit current at its terminal, in parallel with a resistor with the value equal to the equivalent resistance of the network. The equivalent resistance of a two terminal network is equal to the open circuit voltage divided by the short circuit current. Experimentally Thevenins resistance can be found by progressively loading the circuit until its output voltage drops to half the open circuit voltage. At that point the load resistance is equal to the Thevenins resistance.

In electrical circuit theory, Thevenin's Theorem for linear electrical networks states that any combination of voltage sources, current sources and resistors with terminals is electrically equivalent of a single voltage source V and a single series resistor R.

This theorem states that a circuit of voltage source and resistors can be converted into a Thevenins equivalent, which is simple technique used in circuit analysis. [17]

For the given network circuit Thevenin's Theorem is verified.

Aim: To verify Thevenin's Theorem.

Apparatus: Resistors, resistance box, D.C. voltmeter, D.C. supply, connecting wires etc.

Circuit Diagram:

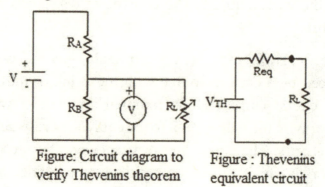

Figure: Circuit diagram to verify Thevenins theorem

Figure : Thevenins equivalent circuit

Observation Table:

Obs No.	R_A (Ω)	R_B (Ω)	Theoretically, $V_{TH} = \dfrac{R_B}{R_A+R_B} \times V_1$ (Volts)	Experimental V_{TH} (Volts)	Load required to get the half experimental V_{TH} Ω	Theoretical load $R_{Eq} = \dfrac{R_A \times R_B}{R_A+R_B}$

Procedure:

1. Using the color code, measure the values of resistors R_1 and R_2 connected in the circuit.

2. Calculate theoretical V_{TH} and theoretical load R_{eq} for each pair of R_1 and R_2

3. Construct the circuit diagram as shown in figure for first pair of R_1 and R_2

4. Then using the resistance box find the value of load (resistance) to get the half value of experimental voltage V_{TH}

5. Repeat the above procedure for other two pairs of resistors.

Viva-voce:

1. What is Thevenin's equivalent?

2. What do you meant by an equivalent circuit?

3. State Thevenin's theorem.

17. Verification of Norton's Theorem

Norton's Theorem is an extension of Thevenin's Theorem. Norton's Theorem for electrical networks states that any collection of voltage sources, current sources, and resistors with two terminals is electrically equivalent to an ideal current source, I, in parallel with a single resistor, R. For single-frequency AC systems the theorem can also be applied to general impedances, not just resistors. The Norton equivalent is used to represent any network of linear sources and impedances, at a given frequency. [18]

Aim: To verify Norton's Theorem.

Apparatus: Resistors, resistance box, d.c. voltmeter, D.C. supply, connecting wires etc.

Circuit Diagram:

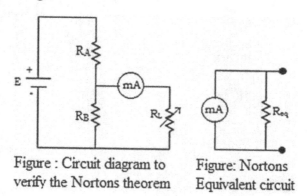

Figure : Circuit diagram to verify the Nortons theorem

Figure: Nortons Equivalent circuit

Observation Table:

Obs No.	R_1 (Ω)	R_2 (Ω)	Theoretical short circuit current, $I_{SC} = V/R_1$ mA	Experimental I_{SC} (mA)	Load required to get the half experimental I_{SC} (Ω)	Theoretical $R_{eq} = \dfrac{R_1 R_2}{R_1 + R_2}$ (Ω)

Procedure:

1. Using the color code, measure the values of resisters R_1 and R_2 connected in the circuit.

2. Calculate theoretical I_{sc} and theoretical load R_{eq} for each pair of R_1 and R_2

3. Construct the circuit diagram as shown in figure for first pair of R_1 and R_2

4. Then using the resistance box find the value of load (resistance) to get the half value of experimental voltage I_{sc}

5. Repeat the above procedure for other two pairs of resistors.

Results:

For the given network circuit Norton's Theorem is verified.

Viva-voce:

1. State Norton's Theorem.

2. What do you meant by an equivalent circuit?

3. What is impedance

18. Study of Electric Energy Meter

A watt-hour meter or electric energy meter is a device that measures the energy consumed in an electric circuit. Its scale is calibrated to give the reading directly in kilowatt-hours or Units. The device may digital or mechanical analog. Fig. shows a sketch of analog energy meter.

The conventional mechanical energy meter is based on the phenomenon of "Magnetic Induction". It has a rotating aluminium wheel called as Ferriwheel and many toothed wheels. Based on the flow of current, the Ferriwheel rotates which makes rotation of other wheels. This will be converted into corresponding measurements in the display section. It consists of an armature that can rotate between the field coils surrounding it. The field coils are connected in series with the load and thus produce a magnetic field proportional to the current in the load circuit. The armature coil is connected in parallel to the load. Thus its magnetic field is proportional to the voltage applied to the load. The combined effect of these two fields is to produce a resulting torque proportional to their product VI. Due to this the armature rotates at a speed which is proportional to VI i.e. the power in watt consumed in the load circuit.

The lower end of the armature spindle carries an aluminum disc, which rotates between the pole pieces of two magnets. The eddy currents induced in the disc, control the speed of rotation. At the upper end of the spindle, a gear arrangement operates the mechanical counter, which records the units. The number of rotations made by the disc is proportional to the number of units (kilowatt-hours) consumed.

Since many mechanical parts are involved, mechanical defects and breakdown are common. The chances of manipulation and current theft will be higher.

Now a day's an Electronic Energy Meter (EEM) functionally performs the traditional Ferrari's wheel meter. One important advantage of EEM is that in non linear loads, its metering is highly accurate and electronic measurement is more robust than that of the conventional mechanical meters. The Power companies benefits from EEM in three significant ways. [19]

1. It reduces the cost of theft and corruption on electricity distribution network with electronic designs and prepayment interfaces.
2. Electronic energy meter measures current in both Phase and Neutral lines and calculate power consumption based on the larger of the two currents.
3. It improves the cost and quality of electricity distribution.

Aim: To study the working and billing of electric energy meter.

Apparatus: Electric Energy meter fitted on the wooden board, Heater, high wattage bulbs, well insulated connecting wires, etc.

Figure:

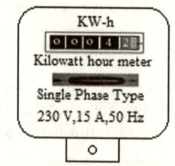

Figure : Electric energy meter

Formula:

1. Electric Energy received by the energy meter = nk Watt Hour

2. Electric Bill in Rupees. = No. of units consumed x rate of one unit.

Energy meter constant K = 2400 rotations/KWh.

$$= 1/2.4 = 0.4166 \text{ Wh/rotations.}$$

Observation Table:

Initial reading (A)	No. of rotations of disc (n)	Time for n rotations (t min)	Final reading (B)	Units consumed B - A	Electric energy received = nk (Watt-hours)	Power recorded nk/t watts.

Procedure:

1. Note the initial energy meter scale reading.

2. Make the connections as shown in the figure. Switch on the supply.

3. As the disc of the watt-hour meter begins to rotate. Count the number of rotations for a known time say 20 minutes measured accurately by stopwatch. Record the time and number of rotations.

4. Switch off the mains and again repeat the procedure for another two observations for the same load appliance.

Switch off the mains. Disconnect the first appliance. Connect the second appliance and repeat the whole procedure again taking three observations.

Note: Do not touch anything with naked hands while performing the experiment.

Switch off the mains supply before handling.

Results:
1. The working of electrical energy meter is studied.
2. The billing procedure of energy meter is worked and the bill for one month is ....

Viva-voce:
1. Define a kilowatt-hour.
2. What is electric energy meter?
3. What the disc of energy meter rotates?
4. What is eddy current?

5. An electric iron is marked 750W-250V. What does it mean?

6. At present what is rate of electric power supplied by M.S.E.B.?

19. Energy gap of semiconductor diode

Band theory of solids:

A useful way to visualize the difference between conductors, insulators and semiconductors is to plot the available energies for electrons in the materials. Instead of having discrete energies as in the case of free atoms, the available energy states form bands. Crucial to the conduction process is whether or not there are electrons in the conduction band. In insulators the electrons in the valence band are separated by a large gap from the conduction band, in conductors like metals the valence band overlap the conduction band, and in semiconductors there is a small enough gap between the valence and conduction bands that thermal or other excitations can bridge the gap. With such a small gap, the presence of a small percentage of a doping material can increase conductivity dramatically.

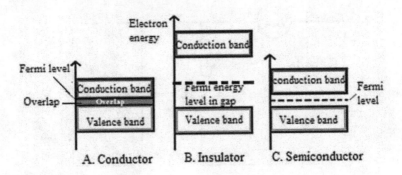

In conductors, there is no band gap sine the valence band overlaps the conduction band. The large energy gap between the valence and conduction bands in an insulators means at ordinary temperatures, no electrons can reach the conduction band.[20, 21]

In semiconductors, the band is small enough that the thermal energy can bridge the gap for a small fraction of the electrons.

An important parameter in the band theory is the Fermi level, the top of the available electron energy levels at low temperatures. The position of the Fermi level with the relation to the conduction band is a crucial factor in determining electrical properties.

Aim: To determine the energy gap of the given semiconductor diode.µ

Apparatus: Semiconductor diode, micro-ammeter (0-10V), 12 V D.C supplies, Rheostat, etc.

Diagram:

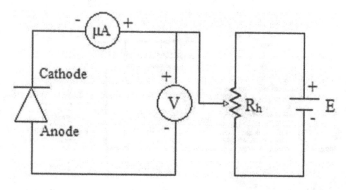

Observation Table:

Obs no.	Temperature	T = t + 273 (°K)	1/T	Current I	Log I

Formulae:

$$\mathrm{Log_{10}I = Log_{10}A - \frac{Eg}{[2(2.303)KT]}}$$

Where, Eg – the energy gap,

$Eg = \text{Slope} \times 4.606 \times 8.467 \times 10^{-5}$ eV

K = Boltzmann constant = 8.467×10^{-5} and T = Absolute temperature.

Calculation and graph:

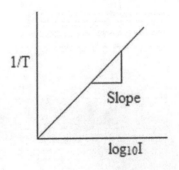

Viva-voce:

1. What is an energy band in a solid?

2. What is a valence band?

3. What is conduction band?

4. What is energy gap or energy band gap?

Practical Physics for undergraduates

5. What is the order of energy gap in a semiconductor?
   Ans. 1eV

6. At what temperature would an intrinsic semiconductor behave like a perfect insulator?

20. I-V Characteristics of Photo cell.

The Photoelectric Effect:

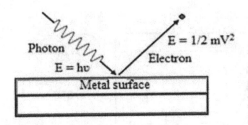

The remarkable aspects of the photoelectric effect are as below.

There are no time lags, i.e. the electrons were emitted immediately.

Increasing the intensity of the light increased the number of photoelectrons, but not their maximum kinetic energy.

Red light will not cause the ejection of electrons, no matter what the intensity!

A weak violet light will eject only a few electrons, but their maximum kinetic energies are greater than those for intense light of longer wavelengths!

It is clear from the photoelectric experiment, that the energy of the ejected electrons is proportional to the frequency of the illuminating lights. This showed that the ejection of the electrons energy is proportional to light frequency. [22]

Aim: To study the Voltage-Current characteristics of photo cell.

Apparatus: Photo electric cell, DC power supply (-30V), voltmeter (0-30V), micro ammeter (0-100-A), meter scale etc.

Figure:

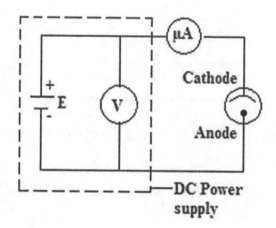

Observation Table:

Obs No.	Current I (A)	Distance between source and photocell (d) (for 10v)	$1/d^2$ (for 10 v)	Distance between source and photocell (d) (for 30 v)	$1/d^2$ (for 30 v)

For constant distance: D = _____ cm.

Obs no.	Voltage (V)	Current (I)	Obs no.	Voltage (V)	Current (I)

Calculation and graphs:

1. Plot the graph of I against $1/d^2$
2. Plot the graph of I against V at constant distance.

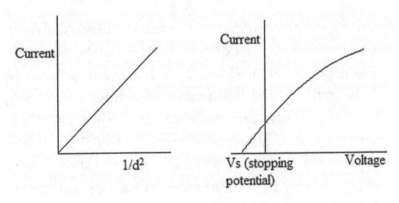

Calculations and result:
Viva-voce:

1. What is photo-electric effect?
2. How many elements photocell consists?
3. What do you mean by inverse square law?
4. What is stopping potential? What is the difference between photodiode and photocell?

21. Lissajous figure using C.R.O.

When two different frequencies that are in phase with each other are applied to the horizontal and vertical inputs of an oscilloscope or channels 1 and 2 of a dual beam oscilloscope and the ratio of the frequencies is a ratio of integers, stationary patterns are observed on the screen. These patterns are called Lissajous patterns (In 1860, Frenchman, Lissajous investigated). Lissajous went on to study sound waves produced by a tuning fork in contact with water, and in 1855 he found a way of studying acoustic vibration by reflecting a light beam from a mirror attached to a vibrating object onto a screen. He set up two tuning forks at right angles, with one vibrating at twice the frequency of the other, and found that the curved lines would combine to make a figure of eight pattern. Some typical Lissajous patterns are shown above. [23]

Aim: To obtain the Lissajous figure using C.R.O.

Apparatus: C.R.O., function generators, connecting wires etc.

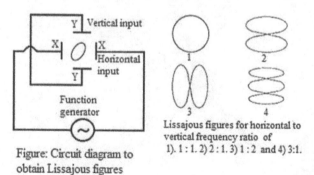

Figure: Circuit diagram to obtain Lissajous figures

Lissajous figures for horizontal to vertical frequency ratio of
1). 1 : 1. 2) 2 : 1. 3) 1 : 2 and 4) 3:1.

Procedure:

Connect one of the audio generators to the input-1 (the x or horizontal input) of the oscilloscope.

Adjust the frequency of the audio generator to 50Hz, set the sine wave switch to since, and the output control to midway.

Connect the other audio generator to the input-2 (the y or vertical input) and adjust its frequency to 50Hz and the sine wave switch to sine as for the other audio generator.

When both frequencies are equal you will get a single lissajous figure, as shown in figure.

Now keep one frequency constant and vary another frequency, from 100 to 300Hz. Record the lissajous figures.

Obtain the different Lissajous patterns shown above. In each case measure the frequency of the second audio generator and enter the values in the table below. The frequency of the first audio generator must remain at 50 Hz throughout the experiment.

Constant frequency F_1(50Hz)	Frequency F_2	F_2/F_1	Pattern on the screen	Standard frequency F_1(50 Hz)	Frequency F_1	F_1/F_2	Pattern on the screen
50	50	1	⃝			1	⃝
50	100	2	∞			2	∞
50	150	3	⫳			3	⫳

22. Thermistor characteristics.

Electric-based temperature sensors i.e. thermistor and thermocouple are mostly used due to their higher accuracy and ease in providing measurements. These sensors are based on the principle of change of electrical resistance or voltage of some material in a reproducible manner with temperature.

Resistance temperature Detector (RTD):

The variation of resistance R of an RTD with temperature T for most metallic materials can be expressed as

$$R(T) = R_0[1 + \alpha_1(T-T_o) + \alpha_2(T-T_0)^2 + \text{------}] \text{---------} (1)$$

Where T_o is a reference temperature, R_0 is the resistance at the reference temperature, and the α_is are some positive constant coefficients. The number of the terms included in equation 1 depends on the material and required accuracy. Typically, only α_1 is used since linearity can be achieved over a wide range of temperatures. Platinum, for example, is linear within ± 0.4% over the range of -100⁰ to 300⁰ F. Semiconductor resistance temperature sensors (thermistor) are more sensitive than RTDs. They have very large negative coefficient, and a highly nonlinear characteristic. Their resistance/temperature relationship is,

$$R = R_0 \exp[\beta(\frac{1}{T} - \frac{1}{T_0})]$$

Where T and T_0 are absolute temperatures in Kelvin and R (R_0) is the resistance of the material at temperatures T and (T_0). The reference temperature T_0 is generally taken at 298^0 K. The constant coefficient β ranges from 3500^0 to 4600^0 K depending on the material, temperature and individual construction for each sensor; therefore, it must be determined for each thermistor. Thermistors exhibit large resistance changes with temperature. [24]

Aim: To determine the temperature coefficient of a thermistor.

Apparatus: Thermistor, heater, oil bath, post Office Box, galvanometer, battery etc.

Figure:

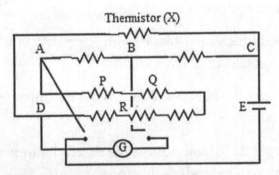

Figure: Circuit diagram to find the temeprature coefficient using Thermistor.

Observation table (1):

Obs No.	P (Ω)	Q (Ω)	R (Ω)	$X = \frac{Q}{P} \times R$	Mean X (Ω)
1					
2					

Observation table (2):

Obs no	Temp °C	Resistance X (Ω)	Log X	T= (t+273) K	1/T

Formulae: Temperature Co-efficient of Thermistor is given as,

$A = -b/T^2$, where b is the constant of Thermistor. T, the specific temperature, i.e. for room temperature.

Procedure:

1. Connect the circuit as per the circuit diagram.
2. Take some resistances from p and Q of the P.O.B. the galvanometer will show deflection.
3. Now withdraw resistance from R so that you will get null deflection in galvanometer.
4. Now apply the heat (till 70°C) to the thermistor through the oil bath.
5. Withdraw the resistances at the desired temperature so that you will get null deflection.
6. Repeat step 5 for different temperatures.
7. Plot the graph of $\log_e x$ versus $1/T$, find the constant 'a' and 'b'.

23. Planks constant by photo cell.

Planck's constant (h), a physical constant was introduced by Germen physicist named Max Planck in 1900. The significance of Planck's constant is that 'quanta' (small packets of energy) can be determined by frequency of radiation and Planck's constant. It describes the behavior of particle and waves at atomic level as well as the particle nature of light.

Light comes in discrete plackets, called photons, each with an energy proportional to its frequency, $E = h\upsilon$. For each metal, there exists a minimum binding energy for an electron characteristic of the element, also called the work function (W_0). When a photon strikes a bound electron it transfers its energy to the electron. If this energy is less than the metal's work function, the photon is re-emitted and no electrons are liberated. If this energy is greater than an electron's binding energy, the electron escapes from the metal with a kinetic energy (the work function). Expressed concisely the relationship is as such:

$$K_{max} = h\upsilon - W_0$$

This maximum kinetic energy can be determined by applying a retarding potential (V_r) across a vacuum gap in a circuit with an amp meter. On one side of this gap is the photo electron emitter, a metal with work function W_0. We let light of different frequencies strike this emitter.

When eVr = Kmax we will cease to see any current through the circuit. By finding this voltage we calculate the maximum kinetic energy of the electrons emitted as a function of radiation frequency. [25]

Calculation and result: Plot the graph of Vs against frequency, by finding the slope calculates planks constant h.

Aim: To verify the Einstein photo electric relation using photo cell.

Apparatus: photo cell, Power supply (0-30 V DC), Rheostat, micro ammeter, voltammeter.

Figure:

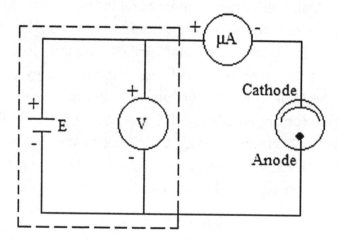

Formulae: The value of Planks constant is given by:

$H = e (V_2 - V_2) \lambda_1 \lambda_2 / (\lambda_1 - \lambda_2)$ where, e = electronic charge, V_1 stopping potential and V_2 anode potential and c be the velocity of light.

Observation table:

Obs No.	Filter color	Wavelength (λ) in cm	Frequency C/λ	Cut-off voltage(Vs)
1	Red	$6460 A^0$	4.6×10^{14}	
2	Yellow	$5890 A^0$	5.0×10^{14}	
3	Green	$5180 A^0$	5.8×10^{14}	
4	Blue	$5050 A^0$	5.9×10^{14}	

Procedure:

Make the electrical connections as per the circuit diagram.

The lamp and scale arrangements are adjusted to get a well focused spot on the zero mark of the scale. The photocell is mounted at one end of the optical bench while place a light source at the same level, nearly 60-80 cm. from the photocell. The light beam should fall on the cathode of a photocell. Now a suitable filter of known wavelength is placed in the path of ray reaching to photocell.

A deflection is observed in ballistic galvanometer .i.e. the spot of light moves on the scale. If the spot moves out of the scale, then it is adjusted on the scale with the help of rheostat R connected in series of ballistic galvanometer. This deflection corresponds to zero anode potential as key K_1 is open. A small negative potential is applied on the anode by closing key K_1 adjusting the rheostat R_h. This voltage is recorded with the help of voltmeter. The corresponding galvanometer deflection is noted by noting the deflection of spot on the scale.

The negative anode potential is gradually increased in small steps and each time corresponding deflection is noted till the galvanometer deflection is reduced to zero. Plot the graph of negative anode potentials on X-axis and corresponding deflections on Y-axis for different filters.

24. Comparison of luminous intensities of two light sources.

The luminous intensity of a light source is the power of light. It is defined in a given direction and is measured in candela; Cd. The candela is one of the seven base units of the SI system and specifies the luminous intensity in one specific angle from a light source. But it doesn't indicate anything about the total amount of light being radiated from the light source.

Aim: To compare luminous intensities of two light sources by photocell.

Apparatus: photo-electric cell, power supply (0-30 V DC), Rheostat, micro ammeter, voltmeter etc.

Figure:

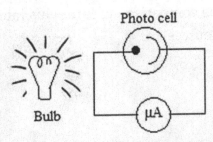

Figure: Experimental arrangement to compare the luminious intensities of two sources

Observation table:

Obs. no.	Distance (d cm) From bulb to photocell	I_1 for 40 W	I_2 for 100w	I_1/I_2
1				
2				

Procedure:

1. Select the source of particular wattage.
2. Take maximum distance between source and photocell.
3. Switch on the light source of 40 watt.
4. Measure the current for various distances.
5. Now switch on another light source of 100 watt.
6. Measure the current for 100W source at the same distances of step 4.
7. Compare the current values i.e. take the ratio, I1/I2 so that you will the comparison of luminous intensities of the given two sources.

25. Use of C.R.O.

The cathode-ray oscilloscope (CRO) is a common laboratory instrument that provides accurate time and amplitude measurements of voltage signal over a wide range of frequencies. Its stability, reliability and ease of operation make it suitable as a general purpose laboratory instrument. The cathode-ray tube is the heart of the CRO is a shown in following figure. The cathode ray is a beam of electrons which are emitted by the heated cathode i.e. negative electrode and accelerated toward the fluorescent screen. The assembly of the cathode, intensity grid, and accelerating anode i.e. positive electrode is called an electron gun. The purpose of electron gun is to generate the electron beam and control its intensity and focus.

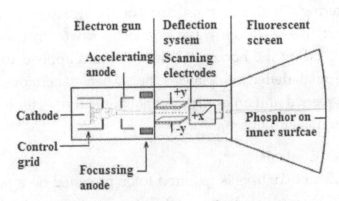

Figure: Schematic of Cathode ray tube

There are two pair of metal plates between the electron gun and the fluorescent screen, one oriented to provide horizontal deflection of the beam and other pair oriented to give vertical deflection to the beam. These plates are referred as the horizontal and vertical deflection plates. The combination of these two deflections allows the beam to reach any portion of the fluorescent screen. Wherever the electron beam hits the screen, the phosphor is excited and light is emitted from that point. This conversion of electron energy into light allows us to write points or lines of light on an otherwise darkened screen.

C.R.O. Operation:

The vertical amplifier is used to amplify the signal which is to be display and then this signal is applied to the vertical deflection plates of the CRT. A portion of the signal in the vertical amplifier is applied to the sweep trigger as a triggering signal. The sweep trigger then generates a pulse synchronized with a selected point in the cycle of the triggering signal. This pulse turns on the sweep generator; kick off the sawtooth wave from. This sawtooth wave is amplified by the horizontal amplifier and applied to the horizontal deflection plates. The sweep generator may be bypassed and an external signal applied directly to the horizontal amplifier.

C.R.O. Controls:

Number of controls is required to be provided on a panel of CRO to facilitate its proper functioning. Intensity control is provided for adjustment of brightness of the spot on the screen. It is accomplished by varying the voltage between the first and second anodes. The horizontal and vertical position controls are provided for moving the beam on any part of the screen. It is accomplished by applying a dc voltage to horizontal or vertical deflection plates. Similarly there are other numerous controls in a CRO, described below.

Horizontal deflection system:
External signal is applied to horizontal deflection plates through the horizontal amplifier at the sweep selector switch in EXT position, as shown in figure. The horizontal amplifier, similar to the vertical amplifier, increases the amplitude of the input signal to the level required by the horizontal deflection plates of CRT.

Vertical deflection system:
The function of vertical deflection system is to provide an amplified signal of the proper level to drive the vertical deflection plates without introducing any appreciable distortion into the system.

Positions controls:
There are two knobs one for controlling the horizontal position and another for controlling the vertical position. The spot can be moved to left or right i.e. horizontally with the help of a knob, which regulates the dc potential applied to the horizontal deflection plates, in addition to the usual sawtooth-wave. Similarly with the help of another knob the spot can be moved vertically up and down, which regulates the dc potential applied to the vertical deflection plates in addition to the signal.

Intensity control:

The potential of the control grid with respect to cathode is controlled with the help of potentiometer in order to control the intensity of brightness of the spot.

Focus Control:

The focusing of an electron beam is done by varying the potential of middle anode with the help of a potentiometer, as shown in figure. By increasing the positive potential applied to the focusing anode the electron beam can be narrowed and the spot on the screen can be made a pin point.

The controls available in most the oscilloscopes provide a wide range of operating conditions and thus make the instrument especially versatile. [26, 27, 28]

Aim: The frequency and voltage measurement using C.R.O.

Apparatus: C.R.O., signal generator, Ac transformer, Rheostat, Voltmeter etc.

Figure:

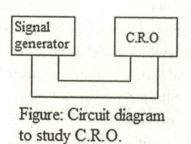

Figure: Circuit diagram to study C.R.O.

Observation table:

1. for frequency measurement:

No. of waves	Time/div (A)	No.of div (B)	Period T=(A × B)/2	Measured frequency, F = 1/T	Actual frequency of source

2. for Voltage measurement:

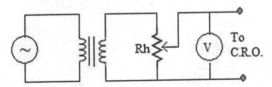

Figure: Circuit diagram to study Voltage measurement using C.R.O.

Obs No.	Amplitude (A)	Volt/div (B)	Measured voltage V = (A × B)/2	Actual voltage (V)

Procedure:

Measurement of frequency:

Apply about 1V, 20 kHz from the signal generator to the Y-input of CRO. Adjust the time base and 'Y' gain so that a wave of 2 or 3 cycles is displayed. Measure the width of one cycle. Repeat the above steps for different input frequency and tabulate the results.

Measurement of A.C. voltage:

1. Apply about 1V, 50Hz from the signal generator to the Y-input of CRO. Adjust the time base and 'Y' gains so that a wave of 2 or 3 cycles is displayed. The amplitude of the wave gives the peak voltage.

2. Switch off the time base and measure the height of the vertical line. The length of the line gives the peak-to-peak voltage. The half the vertical line gives the peak voltage.

3. Repeat the above steps for different input voltage and record the results.

26. Platinum Resistance Thermometer.

Resistance thermometers, also called resistance temperature detectors (RTDs), are sensors used to measure temperature by correlating the resistance of the RTD element with temperature. Most RTD elements consist of a length of fine coiled wire wrapped around a ceramic or glass core. The element is usually quite fragile, so it is often placed inside a sheathed probe to protect it. The RTD element is made from a pure material, typically platinum, nickel or copper. The material has a predictable change in resistance as the temperature changes and it is this predictable change that is used to determine temperature. They are slowly replacing the use of thermocouples in many industrial applications below 600°C, due to higher accuracy and repeatability.

Platinum is a noble metal and has the most stable resistance-temperature relationship over the largest temperature range. Nickel elements have a limited temperature range because the amount of change in resistance per degree of change in temperature becomes very non-linear at temperature over 572°F (300°C) Copper has a very linear resistance-temperature relationship however copper oxidizes at moderate temperatures and cannot be used over 302°F (150°C).

The unique properties of platinum make it the material of choice for temperature standards over the range of 272.5°C to 961.78°C. Platinum is chosen also because of its chemical inertness.

The significant characteristic of metals used as resistance elements is the linear approximation of the resistance between 0 and 100°C this temperature coefficient of resistance is called alpha, a. the equation below defines a its units are ohm/ohm/°C.

$$\alpha = \frac{R_{100} - R_0}{100 R_0}$$

Where Ro = The resistance of the sensor at 0°C, R_{100} = The resistance of the sensor at 100°C.

Pure platinum has an alpha of 0.003925 ohm/ohm/°C in the 0 to 100°C range and is used in the construction of laboratory grade RTDs. [29]

Aim: To determine the temperature coefficient of resistances for platinum using Callender Griffiths bridge.

Apparatus: Callender Griffiths Bridge, Platinum resistance thermometer, Resistance box, reversible key, galvanometer, battery etc.

Figure:

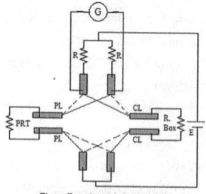

Figure: Experimental circuit to find temperature coefficient using PRT

Formulae:
$$Rt = R_0[1+\alpha t] \text{ and } \alpha = R_t - R_0/R_0 t$$

Procedure:
1. Connect the circuit as per circuit diagram.
2. Insert all keys of resistance box neatly.
3. Switch on the battery; press the key so that galvanometer will show the deflection.
4. Now withdraw resistances from the resistance box till you will get null deflection in the galvanometer. Note that resistance value. Reverse the reversible key obtain the null deflection in galvanometer. Note that resistance value again. This is the reading for room temperature.
5. Place the PRT in the ice bath for 15 minutes repeat the step 4, i.e. obtain the null point, note the resistance value direct as well as reversing the key. This reading is of 0°C.
6. Now insert the PRT in the steam chamber, repeat the procedure of step 4 and Note the resistance value. This is reading of 100°C.
7. Find the value of a using above equation.

Observation table:

Obs No.	Temperature °C	Resistance (Ω)		Mean (R) (Ω)
		Direct	Reverse	
1	Room temperature			
2	0°C (ice)			
3	100°C (steam)			

27. Refractive Index of Prism

Spectrometer is a one of the compact apparatus for obtaining a clear spectrum. It is used to the study the spectra and for finding the refractive index of the material of a prism. The simplest form of spectrometer consists of the Collimator, the Telescope and A Prism Table, as shown in above figure.

The collimator produces a parallel beam of light. Collimator consists of a tube mounted horizontally on the arm of the spectrometer. The tube has a converging achromatic lens at one end and a sliding tube having an adjustable vertical slit at the other end. The focal length of the lens is equal to the length of the collimator tube. The distance between the slit and the lens can be changed. The tube rests on two screws by which it can be slightly tilted up or down if necessary. The silt consists of two sharp edges. One edge of it is fixed while other can be moved parallel to it, by the screw provided at its side.

The telescope consists of an objective lens and an eyepiece. The position of the telescope can be read by two reading windows (verniers) given i.e. V_1 and V_2 which are 180° apart from each other and are fixed to the prism table.

The Prism Table consists of an upper plate and a lower plate separated by three springs through which leveling screw pass. A set of parallel equidistant lines are imprinted on the upper plate. These lines are parallel to the line joining any two of the screws. The prism is always placed with one of its reflecting faces perpendicular to these lines.

To obtain the angle of prism, place the prism on the prism table such that, non refracting surface (base) should be perpendicular to the collimator, faces towards the experimenter. So that light will be incident on both the refracting surfaces at a time. As no way to pass them through the base they get reflected from the same surface and hence get the reflected images through both the surfaces.

To find the angle of minimum deviation, place the prism on the prism table such that the non refracted surface should be parallel to the collimator. The light incident on one of the refracting surface gets refracted and emerges through the other surface, which is the spectrum. The angle between the direction of the incident ray and the emergent ray is called angle of the deviation. It depends upon the angle of incidence. For a certain value of angle of incidence the angle of deviation is minimum and is denoted by δm. If A is angle of prism then the refractive index of the material of the prism can be calculated using the following formula. [30, 31]

$$\text{Refractive index of the material of the prism} = \mu = \frac{\sin\left[\frac{1}{2}(A+\delta m)\right]}{\sin\frac{A}{2}}$$

Aim: To determine the refractive index of material of the glass prism.

Apparatus: Spectrometer, Spirit level, reading lamp and lens, mercury source, prism etc.

Figure:

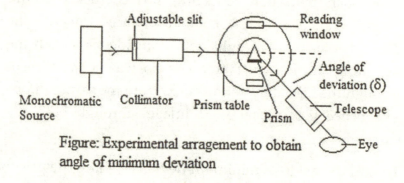

Figure: Experimental arragement to obtain angle of minimum deviation

Formula:

Refractive index of the material of the prism = $\mu = \dfrac{\sin\left[\frac{1}{2}(A+\delta m)\right]}{\sin\frac{A}{2}}$

Observations:

Least count of spectrometer = $\dfrac{\text{Smallest division on main scale}}{\text{Total number of division on vernier scale}}$

$= \dfrac{0.5^0}{30 \text{ divisions}} = 1'$

Observation Table: For Angle of Prism (A):

Obs No.	Vernier used	Spectrometer reading		Difference 2A(degree)	A (degree)	Mean A (degree)
		Right side	Left side			
	V_1					
	V_2					

For angle of minimum deviation δm:

Obs No.	Vernier used	Spectrometer reading		A − B = δm	Mean δm
		For, δm position (A)	Direct reading (B)		
	V_1				
	V_2				

Procedure:

A. For angle of prism:

1. Focus the eyepiece of the telescope on the cross wire.

2. Level the prism table and the spectrometer apparatus using spirit level.

3. Adjust the spectrometer for parallel light by long distance object method.

4. Direct the telescope through an open window towards a sharply defined object at a very large distance. Focus the telescope so that there is no parallax between the vertical cross wire and the image of the distant object. Mark the position of the sliding tube against the edge of the outer tube so that the telescope may be set in the same position if disturbed accidentally.

5. Place the prism on the prism table such that base is parallel to the collimator.

6. Rotate the prism table slowly by some angle till we get spectrum.

7. Make your intension on the yellow line of the spectrum, coincide it with the cross wire.

8. Make (move) the adjustment of prism table and telescope such that the yellow line will go back from the cross wire. At this position note the reading.

9. Remove the prism and take the direct reading.

B. For angle of minimum deviation 'δm'

1. Set the prism to obtain the angles of minimum deviation.

2. Rotate the prism using the positioning while you observe the spectrum through the telescope.

3. Rotate the prism in the direction that reduces the angle at which the light is deviated.

4. Find the position of the prism at which the angle through which the light is deviated is as small as you can make it.

5. Position the cross line of the telescope on the fixed edge of the slit image for each of the lines in the spectrum.

6. Record the angular scale readings from the spectrometer.

7. Reposition the prism on the spectrometer table to orient it as shown in Figure.

8. Repeat the above procedure for this prism orientation.

9. The angle of minimum deviation is half the difference between the corresponding scale readings on each of the two sides.

10. Find the angle of minimum deviation for each spectral line.

11. Calculate refractive index of the material of the prism, using the values angle of prism A and angle of minimum deviation δm.

Results:
The refractive index of the material of the prism is found to be ....

Viva-voce:
1. State the elements of spectrometer.

2. What is the function of collimator?

3. Why you set the telescope for parallel rays?

4. What is minimum deviation?

5. Define refractive index.

6. How does refractive index change with wavelength of light?

7. Which source of light you have used? Is it monochromatic?

28. Beam divergence of the laser

If all the photons are in the same direction then why a laser beams diverges, it would stay that way over a long distance. The perfectly collimated beam with no divergence cannot be created due to diffraction, but it is based on photons rather than wave physics. Due to Heisenberg uncertainty principle $\Delta x\, \Delta p \geq h/2$, one can't really make a quantum have zero momentum in any direction. So it does not means that photons go in the same direction and that's why there is a divergence of laser beam. In actual practice, thinner beam has the higher divergence. [32, 33]

Aim: to determine the beam divergence of a given laser source by Light Dependent Resistor (LDR).

Apparatus: LASER source, LDR, micro ammeter, rheostat, power supply, meter scale Travelling microscope, etc. μ

Figure:

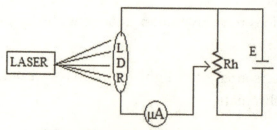

Figure: Experiental setup to determine beam divergence of Laser

Observation table:

Obs. No.	microscope reading	Current (µA)

Formulae: The beam divergence angle θ is given as,

$\theta = \tan^{-1}(d/D)$ Where, D is the distance between the laser and detector.

Procedure:

1. Arrange the LASER source and the detector as shown in figure.

2. Take the 125 cm (D) distance between LASER source and detector.

3. Switch on the LASER source and also the power supply.

4. Incident minimum intensity of LASER source on the LDR. Note down the reading on travelling microscope.

5. Linearly increase the intensity on the LDR measure the corresponding microscope readings, till the maximum intensity.

6. Now the same way note down the reading till you will get the minimum intensity.

7. Plot the graph of current against the distance hence find d.

8. Using d and D find the beam divergence of the LASER source.

Graph:

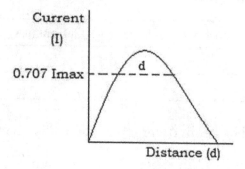

29. Wavelength of the LASER source

The term "LASER" is an acronym. It stands for "Light Amplification by Stimulated Emission of Radiation". So the laser is a device that produces and amplifies light. Einstein postulated the mechanism by which this is accomplished, stimulated emission, in 1917, but only in the last few decades has it been applied. The light the laser produces is unique, for it is characterized by properties that are very desirable, but almost impossible to achieve by any other means.

General Characteristics of Laser Light:

- Laser light is quite different from most forms of natural light. The key differences are, Brightness – lasers have high energy concentration
- Monochromaticity – lasers have a single color
- Collimation – laser beams have narrow divergence
- Coherence in time and space – laser light travels in synchronized waves.

The He-Ne laser is a long tube (glass or steel) filled with a mixture helium and neon gases under low pressure. A solid-state power supply converts 110 volts AC into 1,100 volts DC. This high voltage is applied to a set of electrodes in the laser tube setting up a strong electric field. Under the influence of this field, the gases are activated and a beam of intense red light is emitted from the front of the laser. The light is monochromatic with a wavelength of 632.8 × 10-9 m (6328 A or 6328 nanometers). [33]

Aim: To determine the wavelength of a given LASER source by transmission grating.

Apparatus: LASER source, Screen (graph paper), transmission grating, meter scale etc.

Figure:

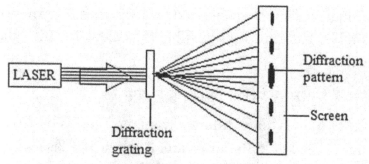

Figure: Experimental setup to obtain the diffraction pattern using grating

Observation table:

Obs no.	Distance (D) cm	Order' m'	Distance between 0 to m^{th} order(Xm)			Wavelength (λ)	Mean (λ)
			Left	Right	Mean		
		1st					
		2nd					
		1st					
		2nd					

Formula:

$$\lambda = \frac{d}{m} \frac{X_m}{[(X_m^2 + D^2)]^{1/2}}$$

Where,

λ - Wavelength of the LASER source.

D - Grating element = $2.54/15000 = 1.693 \times 10^{-4}$ cm

D - Distance between plane of grating and the screen. λ

X_m - Distance between zero to m^{th} order.

Procedure:
1. Arrange the LASER source, diffraction grating and screen as shown in figure.

2. Switch on the LASER source, 10 minutes before start experiment, so that it will hot and emits the uniform beam.

3. Measure the distance between screen and diffraction grating.

4. Mark the diffraction points on the screen (graph paper).

5. Measure the distances of mth order from the center point (zero).

6. Repeat the procedure for another distance between screen and diffraction grating.

7. Make the calculations and find the wavelength of LASER.

Viva-Voce:

1. What do you mean by LASER? State the characteristics of LASER.

2. Why LASER is used in medical field for surgery?

3. What do you mean by wavelength?

30. Double refracting prism

Sunlight and every other form of natural lighting produces light waves whose electric field vectors vibrate in all planes that are perpendicular with respect to the direction of propagation. If the electric field vectors restricted to a single plane by filtration of the beam with specialized materials, then the light is referred to as plane or linearly polarized with respect to the direction of propagation, and all waves vibrating in a single plane are termed plane parallel or plane-polarized.

In 1669, the Bartholin discovered that crystals of the mineral Iceland spar, which are a transparent, colorless variety of calcite, produce a double image when objects are viewed through the crystals in transmitted light. This was the first clues of the existence of polarized light.

Polarized light can be produced from the common physical processes that deviate light beams, including absorption, refraction, reflection, diffraction or scattering and the process known as birefringence which is the property of double refraction.

A majority of the polarizing materials used today are derived from synthetic films invented by Dr. Edwin in 1932, which soon overtook all other materials as the medium of choice for production of plane-polarized light. To produce the films, tiny crystallites of iodoquinine sulfate, oriented in the same direction, are embedded in transparent polymeric film to prevent migration and reorientation of the crystals. Land developed sheets containing polarizing films that are marketed under the trade name of Polaroid (a registered trademark), which has become the accepted generic term for these sheets. Any device capable of selecting plane-polarized light from natural non-polarized white light is now referred to as a polar or polarizer. [34]

One of the light rays emerging from a crystal is termed the ordinary ray, while the other is called the extraordinary ray. The ordinary ray is refracted to a greater degree by electrostatic forces in the crystal and impacts the cemented surface at the critical angle of total internal reflection. As a result, this ray is reflected out of the prism and eliminated by absorption in the optical mount. The extraordinary ray traverses the prism and emerges as a beam of linerarly-polarised light that is passed directly through the condenser and to the specimen.

The amount of light passing through a crossed pair of high-quality polarizer's is determined by the orientation of the analyzer with respect to the polarizer. When the polarizer's are oriented perpendicular to each other, they display a maximum level of extinction. The analyzer is utilized to control the control the amount of light passing through the crossed pair, and can be rotated in the light path to enable various amplitudes of polarized light to pass through. If the polarizer and analyzer have parallel transmission axes and the electric vectors of light passing through the polarizer and analyzer are of equal magnitude and parallel to each other.

Rotating the analyzer transmission axis by 30-degrees with respect to that of the polarizer reduces the amplitude of a light wave passing through the pair, in this case, the polarized light transmitted through the polarizer can be resolved into horizontal and vertical components by vector mathematics to determine the amplitude of polarized light that is able to pass through the analyzer. The amplitude of the ray transmitted through the analyzer is equal to the vertical vector component. If the rotation of the analyzer transmission axis, to a 60-degree angle with respect to the transmission axis of the polarizer, further reduces the magnitude of the vector component that is transmitted through the analyzer. When the analyzer polarizer are completely crossed (90-degree angle), the vertical component becomes negligible and the polarizer's have achieved their maximum determination value. [35]

Aim: To determine the nature of the material of double refracting prism by spectrometer.

Apparatus: Mercury source, glass prism, diffraction grating, spectrometer, etc.

Figure:

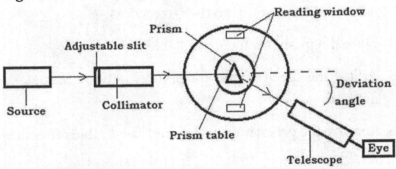

Wavelength of Mercury lines :

Color	Wavelength (A⁰)	Color	Wavelength (A⁰)
Yellow 1	5790	Blue	4360
Yellow 2	5770	Violet	4050
Green	5460		

Polaroid position	Color of spectral line	Spectrometer reading		Angle of minimum deviation A~B (δm)	Refractive Index (μ)
		For δm position (A)	Direct reading (B)		
Ordinary (Vertical axis)					
Extra-ordinary (horizontal axis)					

Procedure:

1. Level the prism table of the spectrometer using spirit level.

2. Switch on the mercury source.

3. Focus the eyepiece of the telescope so that you will get narrow slit, coincide it o the cross wires.

4. Place the prism on the prism table.

5. Adjust the spectrometer for parallel light by Schuster's method.

6. Remove the prism now and mount the double refracting prism.

7. Find the angle of prism. Record it as A.

8. Obtain the double spectrum.

9. Fix the Polaroid on the telescope so that you can see only one spectrum.

10. Obtain the position for angle of minimum deviation for yellow color, record it and then for all other colors.

11. Change the axis of Polaroid, so that you can see the spectrum which was disappear, again Obtain the position for angle of minimum deviation for yellow color, record it and then for all other colors.

12. Find the refractive index for each color.

13. Hence find the refractive index for each color.

14. The crystal will be positive if $\mu o < \mu e$ and negative if $\mu e < \mu o$

31. I- V Characteristics of Solar cell

Solar cell:

A solar cell also called as a photovoltaic cell. It is an electrical device that converts the energy of light directly into electricity by the photovoltaic effect. It is a form of photoelectric cell defined as a device whose electrical characteristic, for example current, voltage, or resistance varies when exposed to light.

Cells can be described as photovoltaic even when the light source is not necessarily sunlight for example, lamplight, artificial light, etc. Photovoltaic cells are used as a photo detector for example infrared detectors, detecting light or other electromagnetic radiation near the visible range, or measuring light intensity. [36]

The operation of a photovoltaic (PV) cell requires 3 basics characteristic:

> The absorption of light, generating electron-hole pairs.

> The separation of charge carriers of opposite types.

> The separate extraction of those carriers to an external circuit.

The photovoltaic effect was first experimentally demonstrated by French physicist Edmond Becquerel in 1839.

Incident sunlight can be converted into electricity by photovoltaic using a solar panel. A solar panel consists of individual cells that are large-area semiconductor diodes, constructed so that light can penetrate into the region of the p-n junction. The junction formed between the n-type silicon wafer and the p-type surface layer governs the diode characteristics as well as the photovoltaic effect. Light is absorbed in the silicon, generating both excess holes and electrons. These excess charges can flow through an external circuit to produce power. [37]

The diode current $I_d = I_o(e^{Avd}-1)$ comes from the standard I-V equation for a diode. It is clear that the current I that flows to the external circuit is,

$$I = Isc - I_o(e^{Avd}-1)$$

Where 'I_{SC}' is short circuit current, 'I_O' is the reverse saturation current of the diode, and 'A' is temperature-dependent constant, A= q/kT. If the solar cell is open circuited, then all of the ISC flows through the diode and produces an open circuit voltage Ioc of about 0.5-0.6V. If the solar cell is short circuited, then no current flows through the short circuit. Since the Voc for one solar cell is approximately 0.50.6V, then individual cells are connected in series as a "solar panel" to produce more usable voltage and power output levels. Most solar panels are made to charge 12V batteries and consist of 36 individual cells (or units) in series to yield panel Voc - 18-20V. The voltage for maximum panel power output is usually about 16-17V. Each 0.5-0.6V series unit can contain a number of individual cells in parallel, thereby increasing the total panel surface area and power generating capability

Aim: To study the Voltage-current characteristics of Solar cell.

Apparatus: Solar cell, Rheostat, voltmeter (0-30V), mili-ammeter (0-100mA), etc

Figure:

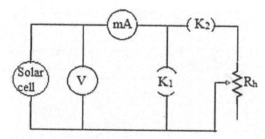

Figure: Circuit diagram to study I-V characteristics of Solar cell

Observations:

Distance between solar cell and source -   -------------- cm

Radius of the solar cell-   -------------- cm

Short circuit current, I_{sc} -   -------------- mA

Open circuit voltage, V_{oc} -   -------------- V

Observation table:

Obs no	Voltage (V)	Current (I)	Power P = VI

Formulae:
- Fill factor: $FF = I_m \cdot V_m / I_{sc} \cdot V_{oc}$
- Area of solar cell = cm^2
- Incident solar power = Power by Suryamapi × area of solar cell = ------- mW.
- Power efficiency = FF × Isc. Voc / Incident solar power.

Procedure:
1. Connect the circuit as shown in figure.
2. Fix the distance between solar cell and source, so that maximum radiations from source will incident on the solar cell.
3. Measure the short circuit current Isc by pressing the key K_1.
4. Measure the open circuit voltage by opening both the key K_1 and K_2.
5. Now press the key K_2 and measure current by changing the voltage ...
6. Plot I-V characteristics.
7. Find the values of Vm and Im from the graph
8. Find the fill factor FF.

Plot the graph, m of I against V

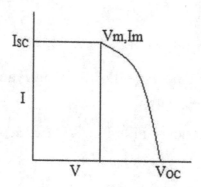

32. Resolving power of grating

Resolvance of Grating:

Resolvance or "chromatic resolving power" for a device used to separated the wavelength of light is defined as $R = \lambda/d\lambda$, where, $d\lambda$ is the smallest resolvable wavelength difference. The limit of resolution is determined by the Rayleigh criterion as applied to the diffraction maximum i.e. two wavelength are just resolved when the maximum of one lies at the first minimum of the other. [38]

Since the space between maxima for N slits is broken up into N-2 subsidiary maxima, the distance to the first minimum are essentially 1/N times the separation of the main maxima.

This leads to a resolvance for a grating.

$$R = \lambda/d\lambda = mN$$

Where N is the total number of slits illuminated and m is the order of the diffraction. [39]

A standard benchmark for the resolvance of a grating or other spectroscopic instrument is the resolution of the sodium doublet. The wavelengths of two sodium "D-lines" are at 5890 A° and 5896 A°. Resolving them corresponds to resolvance. $R = \lambda/d\lambda = 1000$.

Aim: To determine the resolving power of grating by spectrometer.

Apparatus: Sodium source, glass prism, diffraction grating, spectrometer.

Figure:

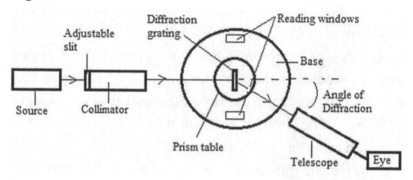

Spectrum Order (m)	Spectrometer reading		Difference 2θ (A~B)	θ	d = mλ/ Sinθ	Mean d
	Left from center (A)	Right from center (B)				
1						
2						

Ist order only	Left from center (X')	Mean X'= a +b/2	Right from center (X'')	Mean X''= a +b/2	X=(X'+X'')/2
Just merge (a)					
Just separate (b)					

Formulae:

Least count of spectrometer = 1'

Least count of micrometer attached to the slit = 0.002cm.

Resolving power of grating = mN, where, m is the order of spectrum and N be the number of lines of per inch on the grating.

Theoretical value of resolving power of grating = $\lambda/d\lambda$. Where, λ be the mean wavelength of sodium (Na) lines.

Wavelength of sodium (Na) lines = 5890 A⁰.

Determination of grating element = $m\lambda = d.\sin\theta$

Procedure:
1. Level the prism table of the spectrometer using spirit level.
2. Switch on the sodium source.
3. Focus the eyepiece of the telescope so that you will get narrow slit, coincide it on the cross wires.
4. Place the prism on the prism table.
5. Adjust the spectrometer for parallel light by Schuster's method.
6. Remove the prism now and mount the grating on the prism table.
7. The procedure for mounting of grating is an follows:

    a. Note down the direct reading.

    b. Add or subtract 90⁰ from the direct reading table rotate the telescope to have that reading

    c. Now fix the telescope rotate the grating table so that you will get reflected image of the slit and note this reading.

d. Add or subtract 45° and rotate the prism table to have that reading.

e. Now the grating is perfectly perpendicular to the collimator.

8. Rotate the telescope to the right so that you will get first order; take the spectrometer reading, hence for the 2nd order. Similarly take the readings to the left side. Note these four readings. Hence find out the value of d.

9. Now mount the adjustable slit on the collimator.

10. Move the telescope to the right side and make the adjustment of just merge and just separate on the first order. Note down the readings, make the similar for right side.

Hence find the mean width of the grating.

References

1. http://www.colorado.edu/physics/phys1140/phys1140_sm98/Experiments/M4/M4.html.
2. http://www.docstoc.com/docs/147549923.
3. http://www.schoolphysics.co.uk/age16-19/Propertie%20of%20matter Surface % 20tension.
4. http://tap.iop.org/mechanics/materials/228/page_46520.html.
5. www.schoolphysics.co.uk/age16-19/Mechanics/Simple%20harmonic%20motion/text.
6. http://academia.hixie.ch/bath/poiseuille/home.html.
7. http://media.uws.ac.uk/~davison/labpage/leedisk/leedisk.html.
8. http://www.education.com/science-fair/article/speed-sound-resonance-cylinder.
9. http://hyperphysics.phy-astr.gsu.edu/hbase/class/phscilab/kundt2.html.
10. http://www.holmarc.com/kundts_tube_apparatus.php
11. http://www.fas.harvard.edu/~scidemos/OscillationsWaves/ReversiblePendulum.

12. http://www.schoolphysics.co.uk/age1619/Electricity%20and%20magnetism/AC%20theory.

13. http://fourier.eng.hmc.edu/e84/lectures/ch1/node6.html.

14. http://www.expertsmind.com/topic/thevenin's-theorems/maximum-power-transfer-theorem.

15. http://www.antonine-education.co.uk/Pages/Physics_4/Capacitors/CAP_02.

16. https://en.wikipedia.org/wiki/Multimeter.

17. http://hyperphysics.phy-astr.gsu.edu/hbase/electric/thevenin.html

18. http://hydrogen.physik.uniwuppertal.de/hyperphysics/hyperphysics/hbase/electric/norton.

19. http://www.gasgoo.com/auto-products/electricity-electronics-298/1219449.html.

20. http://micro.magnet.fsu.edu/primer/java/lasers/diodelasers/

21. http://www.physics-and-radio-electronics.com/electronic-devices-and-circuits/semiconductor.

22. http://www.askiitians.com/iit-jee-atomic-structure/photoelectric-effect.

23. http://fiziks.net/physicsmusic/Experiment%2013.htm.2.http://encyclopedia2.thefreedictionary.com/Lissajous.

24. https://www.fpharm.uniba.sk/fileadmin/user_upload/english/Fyzika/Thermistor.pdf

25. http://labs.physics.dur.ac.uk/level1/projects/script/archive/planck.pdf

26. http://www.ustudy.in/node/3597.

27. http://www.electrical4u.com/cathode-ray-oscilloscope-cro/.

28. http://boson.physics.sc.edu/~hoskins/Demos/CathodeRay.html

29. http://www.evitherm.org/default.asp?lan=1&ID=998&Menu1=998

30. http://www.if.pw.edu.pl/~agatka/lab/prism.pdf

31. http://www.cmi.ac.in/~debangshu/lab1/spectrometer.pdf

32. http://www.cmi.ac.in/~ravitej/lab/r_laser.pdf.

33. http://fas.org/man/dod-101/navy/docs/laser/fundamentals.htm

34. http://encyclopedia2.thefreedictionary.com/Double+Refraction. 35.http://www.answers.com/Q/What_is_double_refraction._describe_construction_working

35. http://www.solar-power-answers.co.uk/basics.php

36. http://encyclobeamia.solarbotics.net/articles/photovoltaic.html

37. http://hyperphysics.phy-astr.gsu.edu/hbase/phyopt/gratres.html

38. http://old.physics.sc.edu/~purohit/704/2013/MorrisonReport.pdf

1. Approximate value of Young's modulus of some materials

Material	Young's modulus (dynes/cm^2)
Nylon	2×10^{10} to 4×10^{10}
Oak wood	4×10^{10}
Concrete	3×10^{11}
Glass	$5 \times 10^{11} - 90 \times 10^{11}$
Aluminum	6.9×10^{11}
Copper	1.17×10^{12}
Diamond	1.05×10^{14} to 1.21×10^{14}
Brass	1×10^{13} to 1.25×10^{13}
Bronze	9.6×10^{11} to 1.2×10^{12}

2. Surface tension of some liquids at particular temperature.

Liquid	Temperature (°C)	Surface tension (Dynes/cm)
Acetone	20	23.7
Glycerol	20	63
Mercury	15	487
Ethanol	20	22.27
Methanol	20	22.6
Water	0	75.64
Water	25	71.97
Water	100	58.85
Acetic acid	20	27.6

3. Viscosity of some liquids:

Liquid/Fluid	Temperature	Viscosity (Poise)
Acetone	25°C	3.06×10^{-3}
Ethanol	25°C	1.074×10^{-2}
Methanol	25°C	5.44×10^{-3}
Water	25°C	8.94×10^{-3}
Water	100°C	5.471×10^{-3}
Olive oil	25°C	0.81

4. The velocity of sound in different liquids media.

Liquid medium	Velocity of sound (m/s) at 25°C
Acetone	1174
Benzene	1295
Castor oil	1477
Ethyl ether	985
Glycerol	1904
Kerosene	1324
Mercury	1450
Methanol	1103
Water	1496

5. Densities of some solid and liquids:

Solid	Density (gm/cm^3)	Liquid	Density (gm/cm^3)
Steel	7.9	Kerosene	0.78
Copper	8.9	Glycerine	1.24
Iron	7.8	Paraffin	0.8
Brass	8.5	Mineral oil	0.8
Hard rubber	1.19	Water	1
Glass common	2.4-2.8	Honey	1.4

6. Thermal conductivity of some materials at 20°C:

Substance	Thermal conductivity (W m^{-1} K^{-1})
Rubber	0.16
Wood	0.16 to 0.4
Silver	429
Gold	318
Glass	1.2 to 1.4
Bronze	0.1 to 0.12
Concrete	0.8 to 2.5

Practical Physics for undergraduates

Obs No.	Depth of orifice inside the liquid (h_2 cm)	Manometer reading		h_1 = A-B cm	Mean h_1 cm
		Upper level A cm	Lower level B cm		
1	a = 2 cm				
2	b = 4 cm				

Practical Physics for undergraduates

Frequency, $n = \dfrac{1}{\sqrt{\rho}} \times \dfrac{\sqrt{T}}{\lambda}$ Frequency, $n = \dfrac{1}{\sqrt{\rho}} \times$ Slope Hz

Obs No.	Mass attached (m gm)	T = mg dynes	Resonating length (1 cm)		Mean (1 cm)	$\lambda = 2l$	$\sqrt{T}$	$\sqrt{T}/\lambda$	Mean $\sqrt{T}/\lambda$
			loading	Unloading					

Practical Physics for undergraduates

Practical Physics for undergraduates

Practical Physics for undergraduates

Practical Physics for undergraduates

Printed in the USA
CPSIA information can be obtained
at www.ICGtesting.com
CBHW032051211024
16187CB00035BA/679